EXPOSING
HATE

PREJUDICE, HATRED, AND VIOLENCE IN ACTION

MICHAEL MILLER

TWENTY-FIRST CENTURY BOOKS / MINNEAPOLIS

To my precious grandchildren,
who I hope can grow up in a world
with a little less hate in it

Twenty-First Century Books
A division of Lerner Publishing Group, Inc.
241 First Avenue North
Minneapolis, MN 55401 USA

For reading levels and more information, look up this title at www.lernerbooks.com.

Main body text set in Adobe Garamond Pro Regular 11/15.
Typeface provided by provided by Adobe Systems.

Library of Congress Cataloging-in-Publication Data

Names: Miller, Michael, 1958– author.
Title: Exposing hate : prejudice, hatred, and violence in action / Michael Miller.
Description: Minneapolis : Twenty-First Century Books, [2019] | Audience: Age:
    13–18. | Audience: Grade 9 to 12. | Includes bibliographical references and index. |
Identifiers: LCCN 2018021233 (print) | LCCN 2018026644 (ebook) |
    ISBN 9781541543911 (eb pdf) | ISBN 9781541539259 (lb : alk. paper)
Subjects: LCSH: Right-wing extremists. | Hate groups. | Hate speech. | Hate.
Classification: LCC HN49.R33 (ebook) | LCC HN49.R33 M555 2019 (print) | DDC
    305.5/68—dc23

LC record available at https://lccn.loc.gov/2018021233

Manufactured in the United States of America
1 - 45127 - 35942 - 10/10/2018

CONTENTS

CHAPTER I

VIOLENCE ERUPTS:
EXTREMISM TURNING TO HATE

In the early morning of August 12, 2017, the usually quiet
college town of Charlottesville, Virginia, was anything but
quiet. A large group was gathering to protest the city's decision to
remove a statue of Confederate general Robert E. Lee, the famous
leader of Southern troops during the American Civil War (1861–
1865). The Unite the Right rally attracted a number of extreme
alt-right, neo-Nazi, and white supremacist groups, all of whom
stand against removing Confederate symbols from the American
South. These protesters support Confederate symbols as a part of
southern culture. They also support the Confederate belief in the
superiority of the white race over other minorities, particularly
blacks. (In this book, *white* refers to people who can trace their
ancestral roots to Europe.) They view removing Confederate
symbols—such as flags and statues—as attacks on the white race.
On this day, they wanted to use the Charlottesville rally to take a
public stand in support of their racial views.

The rally was scheduled to kick off at noon on Saturday. But
rallygoers started arriving at Emancipation Park around eight

The night before the official Unite the Right rally on August 12, 2017, protesters met at the University of Virginia in Charlottesville. The group carried torches and chanted white power slogans as they marched through campus. A small clash with a group of counterprotesters hinted at what was to come the next day.

in the morning. The crowd included a wide variety of extremist groups and militias, or citizen groups organized as a military force. In response, hundreds of counterprotesters gathered. Tensions flared from the very beginning, and rallygoers and counterprotesters yelled insults and chants. Small fights started up and died down. Eventually, a large-scale fight broke out as rally marchers and counterprotesters attacked each other, punching, swinging wooden clubs, and spraying chemical irritants into the crowd. As fighting grew more out of hand, police stepped in to break up the fights and turn people away. The police declared an unlawful assembly, saying it was illegal for individuals to continue to gather because of the threat to public safety and peace. The crowds started to split up, and the Unite the Right rally was canceled before it officially began.

But the violence of the day was not over. One of the rallygoers was a twenty-year-old man from Ohio named James Fields Jr. Fields had a history of violence. As a teen, he had attacked his wheelchair-bound mother several times, once with a knife. He was a Nazi sympathizer and a member of Vanguard America, a white supremacist group that believes the United States should be an exclusively white nation.

At 1:14 p.m. that Saturday afternoon, Fields turned his car toward a crowded intersection where counterprotesters had gathered. Fields plowed into the crowd, sending bodies flying through the air. He threw his car into reverse and backed into more people before speeding away.

Nineteen counterprotesters were injured in the attack. One of them, Heather Heyer, died at the scene. Heyer was a thirty-two-year-old Charlottesville resident and a paralegal with a local law firm. She was also an activist, speaking out against inequality and encouraging her coworkers to be more active in their community to fight for social justice. She died from blunt-force injury to the chest after Fields's car hit her.

The police arrested Fields about 1 mile (1.6 km) away from the incident. They took him into custody and charged him with

Mourners and fellow activists set up an informal memorial to Heather Heyer, placing flowers and tributes of love in the place where she was struck by Fields's car following the Unite the Right rally.

second-degree murder, five counts of malicious wounding, three counts of aggravated malicious wounding, and one count of hit and run. Heyer's ashes were buried in an unmarked, undisclosed location. In October 2018, four alleged members of the California-based Rise Above Movement hate group were arrested and charged with attending the Unite the Right rally and actively promoting violent rioting there.

WHAT IS A HATE GROUP?

Many of the Unite the Right rallygoers, including Fields, were members of organized hate groups. Hate groups advocate hatred and violence toward members of a specific race, ethnicity, religion, gender, or sexual orientation. The hate groups represented in Charlottesville were primarily white supremacists, neo-Confederates, and neo-Nazis. Members of these types of groups believe that whites are by nature superior to blacks and other minority races. They oppose removing statues that memorialize Confederate leaders who played an important role in defending this belief.

Hate groups, however, are not all pro-Confederate or antiblack—they come in all shapes and sizes. The Southern Poverty Law Center, based in Montgomery, Alabama, is a leader in monitoring hate groups across the United States. It defines a hate group as "an organization that—based on its official statements or principles, the statements of its leaders, or its activities—has beliefs or practices that attack or malign [harm] an entire class of people, typically for their immutable [unchangeable] characteristics."

In other words, a hate group is an organization that attacks or harms an entire group of people for characteristics they cannot change. This type of organized hate exists across the United States and around the world—and it's growing. In 1999 the Southern Poverty Law Center officially recognized 457 hate groups in the United States. By 2017 (the most recent year for which data is available), that number had grown to 954 active hate groups.

SYMBOLS OF HATE

The Charlottesville Unite the Right rally took place more than 150 years after the end of the Civil War. In this conflict, the South (also known as the Confederate States of America) fought for its right to exist as a separate nation where slavery would remain legal. The North fought to end slavery and to keep the United States one united nation.

Racism remains a reality in the twenty-first-century United States, and Confederate symbols are controversial. Some southerners claim the Confederate flag and symbolic depictions of famous Confederate generals are an important representation of the South. They feel that removing Confederate monuments undermines the South's history and culture. In some states, it is illegal to take them down. Other Americans believe Confederate symbols emphasize an offensive and violent history of oppression based in slavery, racial discrimination, and prejudice. Since the election of Barack Obama in 2008 as the nation's first black president and with the election of conservative Donald Trump as president in 2016, the debate has intensified.

Violent attacks against black Americans have demonstrated the power of symbols related to race relations in the United States. One prominent example is the 2015 mass shooting at the Emanuel African Methodist Episcopal Church in Charleston, South Carolina, where a gunman killed nine black Americans attending a bible study session. The gunman was twenty-one-year-old self-described white supremacist Dylann Roof. He chose the church for its historical significance as one of the oldest black congregations in the South. The church had also played a meaningful role in the American civil rights movement of the 1950s and 1960s. After the shooting, pictures of Roof posing with a Confederate flag surfaced online. Many Americans were outraged by the connection to acts of violence directly associated with ideologies (belief systems) from Confederate history. In response, many states and cities across the South removed the Confederate flag and other symbols of the Confederacy from public lands and buildings. The tragedy forced the nation to take a closer look at the continued presence of a glorified history of the Confederacy and what it means for all citizens in the South—and of the larger United States.

Hate groups practice discrimination and hatred. They pinpoint specific groups and individuals and often commit violent actions against them. Members of hate groups typically target minority groups. Over the years, various hate groups have persecuted blacks; Asians; Muslims; Jews; Catholics; women; lesbian, gay, bisexual, transgender, queer/questioning, and intersex (LGBTQI) individuals; immigrants; foreigners; and others. Some minority hate groups, though far fewer, target the white majority in the United States.

EXTREMIST VIEWS

The spectrum of political beliefs in the United States is diverse. Generally, political scientists use the term *right wing* to describe conservative politicians who tend to hold traditional views about marriage, religion, family, gender, and patriotism. The term *left wing* usually refers to liberal Americans who tend to have flexible views about marriage, family, religion, and other social norms. Of the two main political parties in the United States, Republicans are generally more conservative than Democrats are. And within each party are differences of opinion, with some members holding more extreme views than others hold.

Hate groups do not represent mainstream thoughts. They promote extremist views. The hate groups at the Charlottesville rally were from the far right of the political spectrum. Their views are so extreme that they do not represent mainstream conservative thinking. The average conservative is not a racist or a neo-Nazi and does not belong to a hate group. Some experts reject the hate group label as biased, preferring the term *extremist group*. Many hate groups themselves also dismiss the hate label in favor of something less negative—for example, Chris Barker, a prominent Ku Klux Klan leader calls his group "more of a civil rights organization."

CHAPTER 2

A LONG HISTORY:
HATE IN THE UNITED STATES

White European peoples began arriving in North America in the fifteenth century. They brought a variety of languages, customs, and religions with them. For example, in the early eighteenth century, Protestant Baptists were beginning to settle in the Mid-Atlantic colonies, including New Jersey, Pennsylvania, Delaware, and New York as well as the southern colonies of Maryland, Virginia, North and South Carolina, and Georgia. In these regions, the Church of England (whose members are known as Anglicans) was already established. Baptists, who also originally came from England, faced open hostility from Anglicans.

The religious differences between the two groups are significant. Anglicans follow a hierarchy of religious rule. They adhere to decisions passed down from higher authorities in the church through the ranks and eventually to churchgoers. Anglicans also baptize their members as babies. Baptists, on the other hand, strictly follow the Bible as the guide for all matters of faith. They think that believers should govern the

The Church of England was integrated into American colonial society by the time of the founding of the new nation. This print, based on a painting by American artist T. H. Matteson, shows Anglican clergyman Jacob Duché opening the first meeting of the Continental Congress (the ruling body of the colonies during the Revolutionary War) with a prayer.

church, not a hierarchy of rulers. They also believe that adults, not babies, should make the conscious decision to be baptized. Because of these differences in faith, extremist members of the Church of England at that time sometimes physically attacked and imprisoned Baptists in their communities. From a modern perspective, these attacks would be considered hate crimes.

In one historic example, leaders of the Mill Swamp Baptist Church, in Portsmouth, Virginia, fell victim to such attacks. Founded in 1719, Mill Swamp was named after the muddy swamps of the nearby Nansemond River. The river was perfect for baptisms, and the Mill Swamp Baptist Church quickly became the most prominent Baptist church in the area.

On a Sunday morning in 1778, the Reverend David Barrow

and church elder Edward Mintz were conducting an outdoor service at the Mill Swamp Baptist Church. A group of Anglicans approached and attacked the two men. A contemporary account recorded that

> as soon as the hymn was given out, a gang of well-dressed men came up to the stage, which had been erected under some trees, and sang one of their . . . songs. Then they took to plunge both of the preachers [in the nearby Nansemond River]. They plunged Mr. Barrow twice, pressing him into the mud, holding him down, nearly succeeding in drowning him. In the midst of their mocking they asked him if he believed, and throughout treated him with the most barbarous insolence and outrage. His companion was plunged but once. The whole assembly was shocked, the women shrieked; but no one durst [dared] interfere, for about twenty stout fellows were engaged in this horrid measure. . . . Before these persecuted men could change their clothes they were dragged from the house, and driven off by these enraged churchmen.

RELIGIOUS HATE IN THE COLONIES

Like Baptists, Puritans were another religious group from England who fled religious persecution in their home country. Threatened by growing attacks on their religion and religious leaders, a group of Puritans fled England for North America. They founded the Massachusetts Bay Colony in 1629. Over the next decade, about twenty thousand Puritans left England and Europe for North America.

The majority of early Puritans were resistant to other immigrants who did not share the same religious views, often denying them entrance to the colony. Puritans persecuted Quakers, for example, who came to North America in the 1680s. Quakers believe in personal communication with God. Puritans, on the other hand, found guidance in strictly interpreting and following the Bible. Puritan members of the Massachusetts Bay Colony expelled Quakers, forcing them to return to England. Quakers who resisted were punished. For example, Mary Barrett Dyer converted to Quakerism in the 1650s. Because of her beliefs, she was arrested, imprisoned, and driven from regions across New England, including the Massachusetts Bay Colony. On a visit to Boston in 1660, she was arrested and hanged for violating a law that banned Quakers from the colony.

Most of the white citizens of early American colonies were members of Protestant churches. They included not only Baptists, Quakers, and Puritans but also Presbyterians and Methodists. Hate speech and hate crimes were common, generally carried out by members of a region's majority religion against members of the area's minority religions.

During the Reformation of the sixteenth century, new Protestant groups split from the Roman Catholic Church. They felt that the Catholic Church and its leadership, including the pope, were corrupt and did not represent the values established in the Bible. Many Protestants were hostile toward Catholics and Anglicans, which share common historical roots and certain religious practices. Anglicans follow the authority of the Archbishop of Canterbury instead of the pope and have a less centralized hierarchy than Catholics.

Throughout the seventeenth and eighteenth centuries, almost all thirteen original American colonies passed anti-Catholic laws. For example, Massachusetts banned Catholic priests from becoming residents of the colony. If they tried to, they risked imprisonment and execution. Georgia and South Carolina offered religious liberty to all colonists "except Papists [followers of the pope]."

ANTI-CATHOLIC HATE

In 1791, ten of the thirteen original US states ratified the first ten amendments to the Constitution, collectively known as the Bill of

Rights. The First Amendment legally grants all American citizens the freedom to practice any religion they choose. The federal and state governments may not legally uphold religious restrictions. However, anti-Catholic bias remained common in the history of the first states. Prejudice was fueled, at least in part, by large numbers of Catholic immigrants from Ireland and Germany in the first half of the nineteenth century. A wave of hate speech and hate crimes were directed at new immigrants and at the Catholic Church.

For example, during the 1830s and 1840s, prominent Protestant leaders such as Presbyterian minister Lyman Beecher publicly attacked the Roman Catholic Church. They viewed the strict hierarchy of leadership within the church, with the pope at the top, as standing against the democratic values of the United States. They also did not trust the church's historic connection to European monarchies (rule by kings and queens). Beecher's 1835 work *A Plea for the West* urged the Protestant majority in the United States to keep

THE FIRST AMENDMENT

Before the United States declared independence, American colonists had limited rights under British rule. The Bill of Rights (the first ten amendments to the US Constitution) was designed to protect individual freedoms. The First Amendment states, "Congress shall make no law respecting an establishment of religion, or prohibiting the free exercise thereof; or abridging [reducing the scope of] the freedom of speech, or of the press; or the right of the people peaceably to assemble, and to petition the Government for a redress [resolution] of grievances."

The leaders who wrote the Bill of Rights intended for these freedoms to limit governmental restrictions on personal matters. It was important to them that citizens be able to practice their religions freely and to say what they mean, including being critical of the United States government, without fear of punishment.

Catholics out of new settlements in the American West.

Anti-Catholic feelings in the United States were strongly tied to the anti-immigrant culture of the era. In addition to disliking and distrusting the Catholicism of new immigrants, many Protestant Americans also feared other changes a new group might bring to the United States. Protestants feared Irish immigrants (most of whom were Catholics). There was a false assumption that they would take away jobs by being willing to work for less pay. Individuals, organizations, and newspapers added to the growing fear by falsely reporting that Irish Catholic immigrants were destroying American culture through public drunkenness and violence.

In May 1844, citizens in Philadelphia, Pennsylvania, rioted in response to false rumors that Catholics wanted to ban Bible readings in city schools. The riots lasted three days. Two Catholic churches and several houses burned to the ground. The riots injured dozens of people and killed at least twenty. Similarly, on August 6, 1855, rioters in Louisville, Kentucky, killed at least twenty-two Irish and German immigrants on that city's Election Day, in what became known as Bloody Monday.

Irish and German immigrants weren't the only newcomers to face prejudice and violent assault in the United States. Chinese immigrants on the West Coast met the same distrust and fear of foreigners. They worked in substandard, unsafe conditions and faced mob violence. In Los Angeles, California, word spread on October 24, 1871, that a Chinese man had shot and wounded a police officer and had shot and killed a saloon owner named Robert Thompson. A mob of more than five hundred white men—at that time 10 percent of the city's population—entered Los Angeles's Chinatown and murdered eighteen Chinese immigrants during the night. Historians think that in the Chinese Massacre, only one of the murdered men was involved in the initial shooting that killed Thompson.

A CATHOLIC PRESIDENT

Religious prejudice continued throughout the twentieth century. Anti-Catholic bias became a significant issue during the 1960 US presidential election. Many Americans feared that candidate (and eventual president) John F. Kennedy, who was Catholic, would follow orders from the pope rather than listen to the American people. Kennedy responded to the concerns, making an important distinction between his religion and his political responsibilities. He said, "I am not the Catholic candidate for President. I am the Democratic Party's candidate for President who also happens to be a Catholic. I do not speak for my Church on public matters— and the Church does not speak for me." Much of the anti-Catholic prejudice faded toward the end of the century, as Protestants became more accepting of Catholics.

John F. Kennedy overcame anti-Catholic prejudice during his campaign to become the thirty-fifth president of the United States. In this 1960 photo, he speaks to a large crowd at one stop along his campaign trail.

HATRED TOWARD BLACK AMERICANS

Black Americans have faced hatred, discrimination, and violence since they were first brought to the United States as an enslaved people in the seventeenth century. Slavery was legal in the American colonies and especially practiced throughout the American South. It was in place informally in many other parts of the colonial world and in those same areas after the United States became an independent nation in the late eighteenth century.

The farming economy of the southern states rested entirely on the labor of enslaved peoples. In the early nineteenth century, the white abolitionist movement emerged among social reformers such as William Lloyd Garrison and writers such as Harriet Beecher Stowe. They urged the emancipation (freeing) of slaves. But many southerners feared emancipation would cripple if not destroy their economy and the southern way of life. To defend slavery, thirteen southern states seceded (separated) from the Union in the early 1860s, and in 1861 the Civil War began.

The Union (Northern) army won the war. The Thirteenth Amendment to the Constitution officially abolished slavery in the United States in 1865. Yet the cultural structures and attitudes that had supported slavery were deeply engrained in the fabric of the nation. They influenced laws and a social system that continued to discriminate against and persecute black Americans.

When slavery was legal, plantation owners hired slave catchers to hunt down and bring back runaway slaves. If a slave was found, a slave catcher had the legal right to bring that person back to the plantation, where that person would be brutally beaten, whipped, or lynched (murdered and strung up, often naked, from a tree for all to see). After the Civil War, white Americans continued this type of organized violence to intimidate black Americans. The goal was to prevent black people from exercising their new freedom and rights, including the right to vote, buy land, and pursue an education. White lynch mobs would seek black victims, often accusing them of crimes they hadn't committed.

INSTITUTIONALIZED RACISM

Racism and the legacy of slavery impact modern American everyday life. Through institutionalized racism, race-based prejudice and discrimination are woven throughout social, business, and government institutions. Institutional racism affects the daily lives of many black Americans and is often less perceptible than racism directed against specific individuals. Black Power activist Kwame Ture, known at the time as Stokely Carmichael, noted in 1967 that this type of racism is "less overt, far more subtle" than individual acts of prejudice and hate—but no less harmful.

Law enforcement and security organizations are statistically more likely to target people of color. And people of color are more likely to face violence from police during encounters. Despite making up only 2 percent of the US population, black males aged fifteen to thirty-four make up roughly 15 percent of all deaths due to the deadly use of force by police officers.

Black people are three times more likely to be arrested for marijuana-related offenses than white people are, even though both groups use and sell drugs at similar rates. Prosecutors are more likely to dismiss or reduce relatively minor charges against white defendants than they are to do so for black defendants. And black men convicted on federal charges receive 19 percent longer sentences than white men convicted of the same crimes.

Racial minorities are statistically underrepresented in positions of political power. The 115th US Congress, sworn into office on January 3, 2017, contains the widest diversity of any previous group of representatives. Yet women and racial minorities still make up less than 20 percent of all lawmakers, and 9.4 percent of members are black.

Institutional racism plays out in the representation of race in pop culture as well. For example, black women are more highly sexualized in ads, movies, and music videos than are white women. People of color are also more likely to be shown as bad people than as positive authority figures in movies and television shows. In these many ways, institutionalized racism supports and promotes prejudice and hatred toward marginalized groups.

They would often beat these victims to death and then hang them from a tree by a noose around the neck.

Lynching was a horrifying and everyday reality. According to reports from the *Chicago Tribune*, white mobs lynched 3,337 black Americans between 1882 and 1903. During the single year of 1892, white mobs lynched 200 black Americans. Members of that era's main hate group, the Ku Klux Klan, carried out many of these lynchings.

In 1925 and 1926, at the height of the KKK's membership, klansmen from across the United States gathered in Washington, DC. During these "konklaves," tens of thousands of members marched down Pennsylvania Avenue from the Capitol Building.

KU KLUX KLAN

On Christmas Eve 1865 in Pulaski, Tennessee, a group of Confederate Civil War veterans met in secret. Their mission? To form a secret society to reverse the new laws that gave a range of rights to formerly enslaved black Americans. These men in Pulaski believed in white racial superiority—that the white race is superior to all others, especially blacks. They called their group the Ku Klux Klan (KKK), a name roughly translated from multiple languages to "circle of brothers." This small group quickly grew and transformed from an informal social group to a large paramilitary (unofficial armylike) organization.

The KKK used various forms of violence to intimidate black Americans and to influence lawmakers to maintain white supremacy. Nighttime Klan raids, called night rides, terrorized black citizens. The

KKK would burn down the houses of black families. They would beat, whip, lynch, or shoot black people and any allies who challenged white supremacy. The Klan also placed large burning crosses in the yards of their targets, as a tactic to silence them or drive them out of town.

Members of the Klan hid their identities during meetings and raids by wearing white robes and hoods with holes for their eyes. Local law enforcement and judges often looked the other way after Klan members had committed a hate crime. Sometimes they too were members of the group. Klan members typically were not held accountable for their crimes, and any local efforts to fight the Klan were ineffective.

During the early twentieth century, the KKK expanded its mission by attacking immigrants, anti-prohibitionists (those opposed to laws forbidding the manufacture and sale of alcohol), and non-Protestants, including Catholics, Jews, and Mormons. With its broader focus, the Klan spread from the Deep South into a number of northern states, including Indiana, Michigan, Ohio, and Oregon. At its peak in the mid-1920s, the Klan claimed to have between four and six million members. But that dominance didn't last. Various scandals, leadership struggles, and newspaper exposés contributed to the KKK's decline by the end of the decade.

The Klan rose again after World War II (1939–1945) in opposition to the American civil rights movement, which worked toward equality for black Americans. The Klan in this period focused almost entirely on a white supremacist agenda. Members were deeply opposed to supporting and extending the rights of black Americans. Klan members were strong segregationists, resistant to all efforts at integration, or the shared uses of public spaces for black and white Americans. The KKK terrorized civil rights activists and bombed black homes and churches. They murdered black leaders, such as Medgar Evers, an important leader at the Mississippi office of the National Association for the Advancement of Colored People (NAACP). Members of the Klan of this era committed many other violent hate crimes. As the civil rights legislation of the 1960s began to take hold, the group lost members and importance, although it did not completely die away. In the twenty-first century, the Ku Klux Klan still exists but as a small part of wider movements. Experts estimate the modern Klan has between five thousand and eight thousand members nationwide.

THE CIVIL RIGHTS MOVEMENT

As the civil rights movement grew and gained support across the United States, pressure mounted for federal authorities to support civil rights marchers in the South. The marchers protested peacefully in cities such as Greensboro, South Carolina, to integrate lunch counters; in Little Rock, Arkansas, to integrate schools; and in Montgomery, Alabama, to integrate public transportation. At many of these events, protesters faced ugly violence from white mobs and from local police officers. The violence was so intense in some cities that lawmakers called on the president for support from federal troops to dampen the

A group of anti-segregation demonstrators run for safety as police spray them with high-pressure fire hoses during a march in Birmingham, Alabama, in 1963.

violence. Meanwhile, black Americans continued to be the victims of violent hate crimes, including bombings, beatings, and lynchings.

Hate-based violence continued after the passage of the Civil Rights Acts of 1964 and 1968 and the Voting Rights Act of 1965. These laws collectively banned racial and religious discrimination in employment practices; prohibited racial segregation in schools, workplaces, and public facilities; ended discriminatory voting requirements (such as literacy tests); and called for federal oversight of elections in the former Confederate states. The laws also prohibited discrimination in housing sales and rentals. Over time, American society mostly did integrate. However, black Americans continue to face inequality.

HATRED TOWARD LATIN IMMIGRANTS

Organized hatred in the United States shifts its focus across time and depending on demographics. For example, the United States has a long and complex history with its neighbors to the south in Mexico and Central and South America. Some of the tension is due to the long-standing conflict between the United States and Mexico, which dates back to at least the Mexican-American War (1846–1848). During this war, the two countries fought over their common border. By the end of the war, the United States had gained new territory in what had once been Mexico. This included what are now the states of New Mexico, Utah, Nevada, Arizona, California, Texas, and western Colorado.

Yet even with new borders, immigrants from the south made their way to the United States looking for better jobs and a better life. Many came to help build the transcontinental railway in the mid-nineteenth century. But during the Great Depression (a period of economic decline from 1929 to 1942), the US government responded to increasing unemployment by deporting Mexican immigrants to open up jobs for white workers. Agents deported more than two million people of Mexican descent between the 1920s and the 1930s alone. An estimated 60 percent of those deportees were actually American citizens.

BLACK LIVES MATTER

In response to what many viewed as an ongoing pattern of police violence toward black citizens, activists across the United States came together to form the Black Lives Matter movement. The members of Black Lives Matter seek to address institutional racism, especially on the part of police and other law-enforcement authorities.

The hashtag #BlackLivesMatter first spread across social media in 2013 after neighborhood watch volunteer George Zimmerman received a not guilty verdict in the shooting death of Trayvon Martin. Martin, an unarmed seventeen-year-old black teenager, was visiting family in a gated community in Sanford, Florida, when Zimmerman shot him in what many saw as a case of racial profiling. Zimmerman claimed it was self-defense. The Black Lives Matter movement gained traction in 2014 following the deaths of Michael Brown, who was unarmed when he was shot and killed by a police officer in Ferguson, Missouri, and Eric Garner, who died after an officer from the New York City Police Department put him in a choke hold during an arrest. The movement helped to organize protests over these and other racially charged incidents of violence. The movement has been active in civil rights causes and often has a presence at counterprotests against hate groups.

Critics of the movement view it as anti-police and antiwhite. But the Southern Poverty Law Center does not define Black Lives Matter as a hate group. Instead, Black Lives Matter leaders say they "are working for a world

where Black lives are no longer systematically targeted for demise." They do not hate whites or any other group. Their goal is to reduce the violence inflicted on minority populations.

In 2014 a New York City police officer put Eric Garner in a choke hold that ultimately led to his death. On the second anniversary of his death, members of the Black Lives Matter community organized a Stop the Violence rally, march, and healing circle in the South Bronx, a New York neighborhood, to remember Garner and other victims of police violence.

Latinos also faced social prejudices. Mexicans and other Latinos were stereotyped as lazy, unintelligent, poorly educated, and more likely to commit crimes than other groups. Immigrants were viciously attacked as they crossed the border from Mexico into the United States. Once they entered into the United States, Latinos would sometimes be denied access to white establishments. With lower-paying jobs, they often lived in poor areas of towns with other poor Latinos. Mob violence was a real threat to Latinos in the late nineteenth and early twentieth centuries. Experts estimate that thousands of Latinos were killed this way. White mobs would lynch Latino victims after falsely convicting them of crimes ranging from accusations of murder to socializing with or insulting white people. Even children fell victim to mob violence. In 1911 in Thorndale, Texas, Antonio Gómez was arrested for the murder of a white man. When a white mob heard the news, they searched for Gómez, eventually finding and lynching him without a trial. He was fourteen years old.

ANTI-SEMITISM AND THE HOLOCAUST

The rise of Nazi Germany under dictator Adolf Hitler led to World War II. Hitler planned to expand the borders of Germany, and while he was doing it, he aimed to rid the world of what he considered undesirable peoples. First and foremost, he targeted Jews. However, Hitler and members of his Nazi Party also attacked non-Jewish religious minorities, blacks, gay people, Communists, and the physically and mentally disabled. Hitler's goal was to create an Aryan nation, one built on total white supremacy.

Anti-Semitism, or hatred of Jews, dates back centuries. Various countries denied Jewish people citizenship and religious freedom and forced them to live in segregated areas of towns and cities called ghettos. In Russia during the nineteenth and early twentieth centuries, frequent anti-Jewish riots, called pogroms, forced Jewish people out of their homes and towns. Between 1918 and 1921 alone, more than sixty thousand Jews were killed and a half million were left homeless by hundreds of pogroms in eastern Europe.

Hitler manipulated this historical anti-Semitism as a way to bring his Nazi Party to power after World War I (1914–1918). Hitler and his Nazi supporters started by blaming Jews for Germany's defeat in that war. They also claimed Jews were responsible for the nation's postwar economic collapse. In reality, Germany lost the war

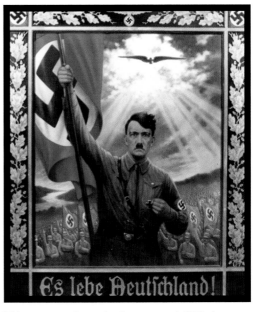

This propaganda poster from around 1935 shows an image of Adolf Hitler in support of the causes of the Nazi Party, including the movement's goal for an Aryan nation. The German words at the bottom mean "Long live Germany."

because it fell short on resources and soldiers over a prolonged struggle. And Germany's economic problems came from the agreement that ended the war. As part of that agreement, Germany had to pay large sums of money to France and Britain, its enemies during the war.

Blaming Jews for Germany's problems was an effective way to unite the country behind the Nazi Party. Hitler gained power in Germany and fueled the campaign to expand the country's political dominance, leading to the start of World War II.

Throughout Hitler's rule, the Nazi government used state-run propaganda (the spreading of ideas for the purposes of helping or injuring a cause) to turn the country against its Jewish citizens. Posters and ads accused Jews of stealing jobs and unfairly controlling banks and other financial institutions. Propaganda described Jews as less morally fit than Christian members of German society.

In addition to dehumanizing the country's Jewish population, the ruling Nazi government also passed laws that discriminated against Jews. Starting in 1933 and continuing through the end of the decade, German Jews faced a growing list of restrictions. More than four hundred pieces of legislation affected all aspects of German Jews' public and private lives. Many of these laws, regulations, and decrees were national. They affected all Jews in Germany. But officials at the local level also placed restrictions on Jewish communities. These laws prevented Jews from holding public office and barred Jews from various public organizations. They also banned Jews from marrying outside their religion and restricted the number of Jews admitted to German schools and universities. To deny Jews political power, the laws stripped Jews of their citizenship and of their right to vote. This hate and prejudice grew into the Holocaust. In this state-sponsored program, the Nazi government and its collaborators in other European countries imprisoned and murdered more than six million Jews plus other "undesirables" before and during World War II. The Holocaust was a hate crime on a massive scale, driven by the Nazis' white supremacist ideology.

LGBTQI HATE

In the post-World War II era, prominent black veterans returning home from war faced bigotry and hate. This spurred the US civil rights movement of the mid-twentieth century. The social activism of black Americans and their allies led to a rise in other identity-based activism. For example, the women's rights movement began to take off in the mid-1960s. So, too, did the movement for gay and lesbian rights. Gays and lesbians in the United States had always faced violent discrimination, and most lived in the closet. Most gay individuals were not open about their sexuality for fear of verbal and physical abuse, loss of their jobs, and shunning by family and friends. In fact, same-sex relationships were illegal in the United States until 2003, when the US Supreme Court struck down the last state law (in Texas) against same-sex relationships. With discriminatory laws in place, police had the right to raid popular places where LGBTQI individuals met. And they did so routinely, arresting and often mistreating patrons and owners. Homophobic (antigay) gangs and individuals burned gay-owned businesses, and gays and lesbians were at risk of being beaten to death.

In the 1960s, the Tenderloin District in San Francisco, California, was one of only a few places where transgender women and drag performers could live openly. But even there, they often faced harassment from police and were arrested for what was then the crime of female impersonation. Gene Compton's Cafeteria was a late-evening gathering place for the area's transgender and drag population. The residents would often gather at the twenty-four-hour cafeteria to relax and gossip. The cafeteria's management didn't like the crowds loitering there and would frequently call the police to clear out the place. One early morning in August 1966, tensions flared to violence when a police officer in Compton's grabbed a drag performer. She resisted by throwing a cup of coffee in his face. The cafeteria erupted into chaos as the customers fought the police by flipping tables, throwing sugar shakers and silverware, and breaking doors and windows.

The action was the first known instance of collective, militant, queer resistance to police harassment in US history. It sparked further resistance from the LGBTQI community, including the well-known Stonewall riot. This act of resistance occurred on June 28, 1969, as police attempted to raid the Stonewall Inn, a popular gay bar in the Greenwich Village neighborhood of New York City. Tired of police brutality, the bar's patrons and neighbors rioted for several days. The protest brought public attention to the historic discrimination against gays and lesbians and pushed the movement for equal rights forward.

Gays and lesbians slowly began to gain rights and protections over the next decades. For example, by 1987, the American Psychiatric

Association had removed homosexuality as a disease from its diagnostic manual. States slowly began to decriminalize same-sex relationships and pass laws protecting gays and lesbians from discrimination in housing, in the workplace, and in other settings. But it was a slow process, and homophobia raged with the onset of the AIDS epidemic in the early 1980s. Acquired immunodeficiency syndrome (AIDS) is the last stage of an infection caused by the human immunodeficiency virus (HIV). The virus weakens a body's immune system so it cannot fight off infections and related diseases. It is typically spread by sexual contact with a person carrying the virus, by receiving a transfusion of blood that contains HIV, or by sharing needles contaminated with HIV. During the 1980s and early 1990s, AIDS disproportionately impacted gay and bisexual men. By the end of 1983, 71 percent of the 3,064 reported AIDS cases were among gay and bisexual men. By the beginning of the 1990s, gay and bisexual men still represented more than half of all AIDS cases in the United States. Many Americans panicked, fearing contamination from toilet seats and casual association with gay men (such things cannot spread HIV). The media sensationalized HIV/AIDS, with alarmist headlines about the deadly "gay plague." In the United States, many men infected with HIV lost their jobs and their homes. Physical attacks targeting gay men surged. Although law enforcement officials did not keep statistics on violence against gay men at the time, some advocates calculated at least a 52 percent increase in attacks on gay men ranging from verbal abuse to murder.

Through intense and unrelenting activism, gay Americans and their allies pushed for money to support HIV/AIDS research. And with that research, advances in health care, medication, and preventive and educational programs became possible. The HIV/AIDS crisis in the United States slowly came under control. This was mirrored by the growth of the gay rights movement and society's growing acceptance of LGBTQI peoples, especially among younger Americans. Legalization

The AIDS Coalition to Unleash Power (ACT UP) was instrumental in advocating to find a cure for HIV/AIDS. The group used public demonstrations called actions to fight for change. This June 1, 1987, action in front of the White House demanded more governmental funding for AIDS research.

of same-sex marriage became an important goal among LGBTQI peoples and their allies, culminating in the Supreme Court's 2015 ruling in favor of the constitutionality of same-sex marriage.

However, as society in general became more tolerant of LGBTQI individuals, opposition has become more radical. Gregory M. Herek, a psychology professor at the University of California, Davis, and an expert on prejudice against sexual minorities, says that anti-LGBTQI individuals and groups "may feel that the way they see the world is threatened, which motivates them to strike out in some way, and for some people, that way could be in violent attacks." Hate crimes against gay married couples, for example, occur—even with the Supreme Court's decision in favor of marriage equality.

ISLAMOPHOBIA

Anti-Muslim hate, or Islamophobia, in the United States is primarily a fear-based reaction to the terrorist attacks of September 11, 2001. During these attacks, nineteen members of the Islamic militant group al-Qaeda hijacked four passenger planes. Two flew directly into New York City's World Trade Center towers. One flew into the Pentagon (the headquarters of the US Department of Defense) near Washington, DC. Passengers and crew on the fourth plane realized what was happening and overcame the hijackers on their flight. That plane crashed into a field in Pennsylvania. In all, nearly three thousand people died in the attacks. The events shook the United States and the world, which had never witnessed a terrorist attack of this scale. As Americans tried to make sense of the tragedy, some began to blame Islam. They claimed, falsely, that Islam is a religion that encourages violence against the United States and other nations of the industrialized West. Experts agree that Islam is no more violent than Christianity. Right-wing extremists such as Dylann Roof—who murdered nine people in the 2015 Charleston church shooting—were behind nearly twice as many terrorist incidents in the United States from 2008 to 2016 as Islamic extremists. However, anti-Muslim groups continued to direct their hate and violence toward the entire Muslim community both inside and outside the United States. (People who practice the religion of Islam are known as Muslims.)

Islamophobia has led to acts of violence, including personal attacks and the burning of mosques (Islamic houses of worship). Just after the 9/11 attacks, hate crimes against Muslims increased significantly. In 2000 the FBI reported 28 anti-Muslim hate crimes. Following the terrorist attacks on 9/11, this statistic jumped to 481 in 2001. The number of incidents dropped to 155 the following year (and has stayed at that level since). However, it remains much higher than in the pre-9/11 world. And since 9/11, the US government has fueled anti-Muslim fervor in a number of significant ways, with policies that

A woman holds a banner against Trump's so-called Muslim ban as part of a protest in Los Angeles in October 2017. The travel ban limits immigration to the United States from several countries with majority-Muslim populations.

focus attention on Muslim individuals and on predominantly Muslim countries. The government ramped up airport security checks for all travelers, and security agents often perform special screenings on Muslim passengers—or on those they perceive as Muslims. Stronger anti-terrorist measures and regulations were enacted. And the US government created a completely new Department of Homeland Security to deal with potential terrorist attacks—with a targeted focus on attacks from Muslim countries. This focus on potential Islamic terrorists has continued into the twenty-first century, with the Trump administration's travel ban on people entering the United States from majority-Muslim countries. This ruling went into effect in late 2017, and the Supreme Court upheld it in June 2018.

CHAPTER 3

ORGANIZING HATE:
HATE GROUPS

In 2015 Europe was in the grips of a refugee crisis. Millions of refugees fleeing wars, poverty, and instability in Syria, Afghanistan, Iraq, and other Middle Eastern and African countries were coming across the Mediterranean Sea into southern Europe. From there, they slowly migrated northward and westward into Germany, France, and Scandinavia. Most of these immigrants were fleeing oppressive, often war-torn regimes. They were seeking asylum (protection as a refugee), a more peaceful life, and economic opportunity.

The response to the refugees varied widely. Some European countries welcomed refugees. Others were openly hostile. Finland was one of the most welcoming, with a long-standing open-door policy toward immigrants. Finland's population of only 5.5 million absorbed an estimated thirty to fifty thousand refugees in 2015. Yet some Finnish residents were opposed to the large number of Muslim immigrants from the Middle East entering the mostly white, mostly Lutheran society in Finland. Protesters railed against what they called the Islamization of their society.

Jussi Halla-aho, a controversial right-wing blogger and member of the European Parliament for Finland, claimed that Somali immigrants were "robbing passersby and living on taxpayers' expense." The country saw a round of protests from anti-immigrant political groups such as Suomi Ensin (Finland First). Anti-immigrant fervor escalated into violence against Muslim newcomers. Finnish officials report that racially motivated hate crimes increased from 919 in 2011 to 1,250 in 2015.

Hard-core Finnish nationalists began to gain strength. They want to preserve ethnic Finn culture, religion, and racial heritage. They fear that refugees from vastly different traditions will bring unwanted changes to Finland, and they fear the loss of national identity. Nationalists pointed to highly publicized crimes committed by refugees and asylum seekers to try to prove their point. One high-profile crime was the March 9, 2015, gang rape of a young Finnish woman by five second-generation Somali teenagers near the Tapanila railway station on the outskirts of Helsinki. The incident shocked the nation. It also spurred discussion of startlingly high and increasing rates of sexual assault by refugees in Finland. According to the Official Statistics of Finland, of the 1,010 rapes reported in 2014, there were three times more immigrant suspects than native-born suspects.

Critics claim that high numbers of rapes go unreported, so the statistics are likely skewed. All the same, several hundred white Finnish nationalists formed a group in 2015 to respond to their concerns about crime. They called themselves the Soldiers of Odin, named after the king of gods in Nordic mythology. The group claimed that Finnish police had lost control of the immigrant population. Members began to patrol the streets as vigilantes (people who take law enforcement into their own hands without the legal right to do so).

Members of the Soldiers of Odin in Tampere, Finland, patrol the streets near a refugee center in January 2016. The anti-immigrant group thinks of itself as an unofficial police force attempting to control the immigrant population.

The Soldiers of Odin movement soon spread from Finland to several other European countries, including Sweden, Norway, and Germany. In early 2016, an American anti-immigrant offshoot group, Soldiers of Odin USA, formed in the United States. These sympathizers met and organized over Facebook. Within several months, the group's Facebook page had more than seventy-five thousand likes, and individual chapters had formed in more than forty-two states. Like the original Finnish group, the American offshoot patrols the streets of US cities, looking for undocumented immigrants, attacking those they find. The members of Soldiers of Odin USA share much of the same anti-immigrant and anti-Muslim ideology of the Finnish group. They oppose immigration in general and are specifically against the United States taking in refugees from Muslim countries. The group's official Facebook page states, "We will not bow down and submit to the Islamization of America. We will defend our rights and our way of life!"

MODERN HATE

The Soldiers of Odin USA is not a unique group. As of 2017, the Southern Poverty Law Center has identified twenty-two explicitly anti-immigrant hate groups in the United States. And hate is on the rise. The center, which tracks hate groups in the United States, reports that the number of hate groups grew by more than 20 percent (from 784 to 954) between 2014 and 2017. And not only is membership in these groups increasing, but they operate more publicly than in previous decades.

Far-right extremists became very active after the 2008 election of Barack Obama as the first black president of the United States. Many Obama critics expressed racial prejudice toward the president with ugly verbal attacks. Some individuals, nicknamed birthers, challenged Obama's citizenship, claiming he had not been born in Hawaii as his birth certificate states. They claimed that as a non-US citizen, Obama was an illegitimate president. (The US Constitution says that in addition to qualifications of age and years of residency, only a "natural born citizen of the United States" can become president.)

Many political scientists and other experts note that during the 2016 US presidential campaign, far-right extremism grew and gained prominence. Republican candidate Donald Trump exploited white supremacist and racist feelings. He pointed to immigrants from Mexico, describing them as rapists and murderers. He blamed immigration in general for taking away jobs from white Americans. During his campaign, he was accused of past sexual harassment and other forms of discrimination against and objectification of women. Former Trump aide Omarosa Manigault Newman later claimed he treated women differently than men because he "believes [women] are beneath him." During his campaign, Trump made disparaging remarks

Donald Trump spoke at a campaign rally in Phoenix, Arizona, in July 2015 during his run for US president. In front of a large, cheering crowd, he spoke of his determination to turn back undocumented immigrants to the United States, particularly from Latin American and Middle Eastern nations.

about Muslims, at one point claiming, "I think Islam hates us." He suggested that he might support the creation of a database that tracks Muslims in the United States. Alt-right groups and conservative media outlets support and voted for Trump. When he won the election and took office, these groups moved even more into the mainstream. For example, Trump appointed several prominent figures who were leaders in the alt-right movement to his administration. They included Steve Bannon (former executive chairman of alt-right Breitbart News) and Sebastian Gorka (who has ties to anti-Semitic groups in his native Hungary). Since his election, Trump has also retweeted links and memes from alt-right sources.

Kevin Boyle, a professor of American history at Northwestern University in the Chicago area, says, "Donald Trump gave [white supremacists] permission to come out into the real world." This was immediately noticeable the day after Trump won the November 8, 2016, presidential election. On November 9, the number of reported hate crimes in the United States jumped from 10 to 27. According to the FBI, November 9 had the most hate crimes of any other day that year. The number of hate crimes for the entire year of 2016 increased from 5,850 in 2015 to 6,121.

Many social scientists see a connection between Trump's words and actions and hate crimes. A study by two researchers from the University of Warwick in Coventry, England, indicates that when Trump tweets about Muslims or Islam, a corresponding increase in anti-Muslim hate crimes occurs. Madihha Ahussain is an attorney at Muslim Advocates, an organization that provides civil rights education and legal help in the fight for justice for Americans of all faiths. She says, "Whether it's a tweet or whether it's in a policy [Trump is] introducing, or if it's in a policy someone in his administration is introducing . . . it all comes together to create this kind of environment where targeting Muslims is acceptable or has become acceptable."

CODED LANGUAGE

Some observers note that Trump's word choices sometimes acknowledge and support the views of the alt-right, particularly when he is speaking about minority groups. For example, he often uses coded language to talk about people of color. This type of speech uses phrases that are negatively and historically tied to specific groups of people. The language usually has racist or offensive connotations. Some examples of coded Trump language include calling black protesters "thugs" and Latino immigrants "animals." Ian Haney López, professor of law and author of *Dog Whistle Politics: How Coded Racial Appeals Have Reinvented Racism and Wrecked the Middle Class*, explains, "Current racial code operates by appealing to deep-seated stereotypes of groups that are perceived as threatening. But they differ from naked racial terms in that they don't emphasize biology—so it's not references to brown skin or black skin." Coded language, then, makes racist statements more subtle than other forms of direct racial slurs.

IDENTIFYING HATE GROUPS

With the rise in hate speech and hate violence in the United States, many Americans are wondering, How do hate groups form? Some groups spring up in response to like-minded individuals meeting locally. Or, like the Soldiers of Odin USA, they may meet online. Others are inspired by groups elsewhere in the country or around the world. They may set up an official or unofficial offshoot of an existing group. Groups can also form after splitting from existing groups. A member of a group may offshoot, leaving one group to form and lead a similar group. Some new hate groups come from resurrections, where members form a group around the remains of an older group that has died out. These new leaders may bring back the old group or just its name. And some new groups are local branches connected to a larger national group. Sometimes a group will form around an issue and become extremist over time.

How can you identify a hate group? Hate groups have an organized structure with some sort of membership process. This often requires that members pay dues or suggested "donations," and members participate in activities such as meetings or rallies. Many of these groups communicate with members through mailing lists, social media groups, or a formal website. Larger organizations may have many smaller chapters.

Understanding a group's messaging is another key way of identifying whether it is truly a hate group. Some hate groups openly promote hostile or violent behavior toward one or more social groups. Other hate groups are more difficult to spot. For example, a hate group may have a positive message about its goals. The group may emphasize patriotism or protecting vulnerable members of society. However, despite its positive messaging, the hate group will also have a bias against specific groups of people. The bias is typically against nonwhite, non-Christian peoples. According to the Southern Poverty Law Center definition, a hate group not only opposes a specific group of people, but it also attacks that group or groups. Members of a hate group typically believe that individuals of the target group are inferior and that those people threaten an ideal way of life. Members of the hate group will treat those people with contempt, hatred, and violence.

MONITORING HATE

The Anti-Defamation League, based in New York City, and the Southern Poverty Law Center in Montgomery, Alabama, are two major organizations that identify and track hate groups in the United States. Law enforcement agencies, the media, and researchers often turn to data from these organizations to monitor extremism in the United States.

The B'nai B'rith Jewish service organization founded the Anti-Defamation League in 1913. Its mission was "to stop the defamation [targeted and manipulated speech that injures the reputation of a person or people] of the Jewish people, and to secure justice and fair treatment to all." The organization has since moved beyond a focus on anti-Semitism to include all forms of hate. The organization's work has led to the development of a branch of criminal law devoted specifically to hate crimes.

Through its Center on Extremism, the Anti-Defamation League monitors all forms of extremism, terrorism, and hate. Its staff provides information, training, and other resources about hate groups to law enforcement, communities, and other organizations. They also maintain a database that tracks the slogans, graphics, and symbols of various hate groups around the world.

Morris Dees and Joe Levin, two Alabama lawyers, founded the Southern Poverty Law Center in 1971 as a civil rights law firm. The firm helped victims of hate group violence file civil lawsuits—suits focusing on the right of individuals or organizations to hold another person or party responsible for a crime committed against them. Typically, a successful claim will lead to a payment of money to the victim or victims. In 1986 the organization shifted its focus from civil rights work to fighting right-wing extremism in all its forms.

The Southern Poverty Law Center has become a leading organization in monitoring hate groups and extremists. The organization tracks the activities of more than fifteen hundred extremist groups in the United States. It also has a database of hate groups called the Extremist Files and posts an online map of hate groups operating across the United States. Like the Anti-Defamation League, the center also provides anti-hate resources for law enforcement officials and other organizations.

Several local and national governmental organizations also play a key role in monitoring and tracking hate crimes. In particular, the FBI gathers hate crime statistics from law enforcement organizations across the country to create a massive database of reported hate crimes. The FBI relies on this database in its role as the lead agency in investigating criminal violations of federal civil rights laws. Local FBI offices also participate with community groups and law enforcement agencies in local Hate Crime Working Groups that develop strategies to deal with local hate crime issues.

These hate-monitoring organizations have their critics. The Anti-Defamation League has been accused of Islamophobia and has been criticized for labeling the Black Lives Matter movement as anti-Semitic. Both charges are complex, and not all Americans support the organization. The Southern Poverty Law Center has faced backlash for labeling right-leaning, mainstream groups and individuals as hate groups and extremists. Some critics say that while these groups are very conservative, they do not deserve or qualify for the hate group label. And many people criticize the FBI's hate crime database, claiming that it relies too heavily on self-reporting from local and federal agencies. These critics point out that self-reporting often soft-pedals the seriousness of a situation and does not provide an accurate number of hate crimes, typically underreporting them. Double-checking data from multiple sources is the best way to ensure that information is dependable. If data is consistent among the organizations, it is usually reliable.

WHERE ARE HATE GROUPS LOCATED—AND WHY?

Hate groups are in communities big and small all across the United States. Most groups are small and local, with larger groups split into local cells or chapters. Local chapters are often the most successful at recruiting, which they usually do person-to-person. It's also easier to attend a small local meeting regularly than to travel across the country for a large national gathering. So the larger national organizations rely on the internet to connect with local chapters and spread their message.

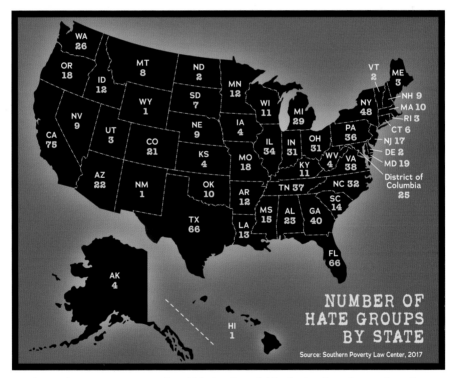

As of 2017, the most recent year for which data is available, the Southern Poverty Law Center has identified 954 hate groups or hate group chapters in the United States. Groups tend to cluster in the southeastern United States as well as in highly populated areas.

As of October 2018, the Southern Poverty Law Center lists 954 hate groups or chapters of hate groups across the United States. While hate groups exist in only about 10 percent of the nation's counties, every state in the nation has one or more hate groups. The center tracks these hate groups on its Hate Map, an interactive online resource on the organization's website.

With the Southern Poverty Law Center's Hate Map, social scientists can see where hate groups form and cluster. Usually, demographics (data about a community and the people who live there) reveal patterns of where and why the hate groups form. The number of hate groups in any area or state generally is greater in highly populated areas. For example, the most populated state in the nation, California, also has the largest number of active hate groups (seventy-five). Less populated states, such as Hawaii, New Mexico, and Wyoming, each have a single group.

The southeastern United States has the greatest concentration of hate groups in the nation. This corresponds to the historical attitudes of the states of the old South and its history of slavery. Social justice researcher Emily Nicolosi says that "people hate for different reasons because US regions have different situations and histories." In the case of the states of the old South, she points to the "history of the Confederacy [and] of discrimination" as contributing to modern southern attitudes toward race, ethnicity, and religion.

Nicolosi and other researchers from the University of Utah in Salt Lake City analyzed Southern Poverty Law Center data and found several factors that contribute to the formation of hate groups. In their 2018 report "Geographies of Organized Hate in America: A Regional Analysis," they found that a region's poverty level was a significant factor in the formation of hate groups. Their analysis revealed that the more people in an area living at or below the poverty level, the larger the number of hate groups. (The US Department of Health and Human Services determines the poverty levels each year for families of various sizes. The poverty level for a family of four in 2018 was set at an annual income of $25,100.)

The average education level of an area also correlates to the formation of hate groups. The University of Utah researchers found that areas with fewer college-educated adults tend to have a higher concentration of hate groups. This correlation is strongest in the South, especially in Texas, Oklahoma, Arkansas, and Louisiana.

The University of Utah research also found that hate groups tend to cluster where there is a larger percentage of whites than of minority races. In these areas, the relatively rare black person or immigrant is more likely to be viewed as a threat to the predominantly white populace. The less diverse an area, the more likely it is to have hate groups with ideologies that focus on white supremacy. "Some people have strong feelings about who belongs, and who doesn't belong in 'their' place," says researcher Nicolosi. "When they see people coming in that they think don't belong, their very identity feels threatened."

WHITE SUPREMACIST GROUPS

Hate groups of the twenty-first century form around issues related to race, gender identity, sexual orientation, and religion. In the United States, the largest number of these groups falls under the general umbrella of white supremacy. According to the Southern Poverty Law Center, more than one-quarter (29 percent) of all known hate groups in 2017 fell under this category. And several other types of hate groups, including neo-Nazi and Christian Identity groups, hold white supremacist views.

White supremacists believe that whites are genetically superior to all other races and ethnicities. They target blacks, Latinos, and Asians. They also believe themselves to be superior to Jews. Many white supremacists view Jews as a separate race, rather than as members of the people and cultural community whose traditional religion is

Judaism and who trace their origins through the ancient Hebrew people of Israel. Many white supremacists believe that white people have a culture that is superior to the cultures of other races. They feel that white people should be dominant in any society. As the number of nonwhites grows in any community or nation, white supremacists fear that whites and white culture are being replaced or threatened. Some believe that the US government itself is controlled by a secret group of Jews and nonwhite minorities. The most extreme white supremacists advocate overthrowing this alleged secret government through violence or terrorism.

Most white supremacists do not act openly on their racist beliefs. But social scientists and other experts say that white supremacists are the most violent of twenty-first-century hate groups. As Jonathan Greenblatt, chief executive officer of the Anti-Defamation League, says, "When white supremacists and other extremists are emboldened and find new audiences for their hate-filled views, violence is usually not far behind."

A 2017 Anti-Defamation League report shows that white supremacists committed 71 percent of the extremist-related murders in the United States over the previous ten years. White supremacists were involved in 59 percent of extremist-related violence over the same period. They have also been involved in terrorist plots and conspiracies, as well as with traditional criminal activity such as burglary, assault, and drug trafficking.

WHITE NATIONALISTS

White nationalists represent a large subset of the white supremacy movement. They emphasize a belief that the national identity of the United States should reflect the dominance of the white race. (A little over 60 percent of the US population is white.) They fear and oppose ongoing demographic changes that lead to more interracial relationships and marriages. White nationalists believe that through racial intermixing, white influence is lost and society becomes intellectually and morally inferior. They want to return to American society as it existed before the civil rights movement of the 1950s and 1960s, when segregation and unequal rights—based on race—were the law of the land.

To accomplish this goal, white nationalists seek to suppress nonwhite races. They would allow immigration only from northern European nations, such as Norway and Germany, whose populations are primarily Caucasian. Likewise, they would like to prevent immigration from Latin American, African, Middle Eastern, and Asian countries. White nationalists share many of the same viewpoints as anti-immigration groups. In fact, some white nationalists, led by alt-right icon Richard Spencer, have a specific goal of creating what they call a white ethnostate. This proposed new nation, to be located somewhere in North America, would allow only white citizens.

NEO-CONFEDERATES

The neo-Confederate movement is another subgroup of white supremacy. It takes its inspiration from the Civil War–era Confederate South. Neo-Confederacy (*neo* means "new") groups idolize the Confederate flag and other symbols of the old South. Neo-Confederates defend the values of the old South, including racial segregation and traditional gender roles. Most neo-Confederates also hold anti-immigrant and anti-LGBTQI views. Many long for the South to secede again from the United States to form an independent nation with closed borders. Other neo-Confederates support white nationalism and white supremacy. Neo-Confederates may also believe in Christian dominionism. This movement claims that God calls Christians to rule over every aspect of society, including government. The largest neo-Confederate groups in the United States are Identity Dixie (Dixie is a historic name for the South) and League of the South. Both operate in the southeastern United States.

RACIST SKINHEADS

Another smaller subset of the white supremacist movement are racist skinheads. At first, skinheads were not a racially motivated group. They formed in England as an alternative to the popular middle-class culture and music of the 1960s. These working-class skinheads listened to music such as reggae and ska—brought to England from recent Jamaican immigrants—instead of mainstream rhythm and blues (R&B). Skinheads of that era, like the skinheads of the twenty-first century, chose to wear close-cropped or totally shaven heads. As a badge of identity, they also favored working-class clothing such as jeans, suspenders, and a white shirt along with heavy boots. By the late 1970s, some offshoots of English skinhead culture were adopting white

The English skinhead music-based subculture of the 1960s began as a nonviolent, non-hate-based movement. Skinheads were easily identified by their haircuts and clothing styles—the fashions of which inspired the racist skinhead movements of the following decades.

power and Nazi ideologies. This was the beginning of the shift to the specifically racist, or white power, skinhead movement. The movement migrated from England to the rest of Europe and the United States in the 1980s.

Music continues to be an important part of racist skinhead culture. Most racist skinheads listen to a type of hate rock music that grew out of the punk rock movement in the late 1970s. Music is still used to recruit new members to the movement. Concerts provide a place for potential recruits to meet members of the larger organization.

Racist skinheads often hold antiblack, anti-Semitic, anti-immigrant, and antigay beliefs. Many of these racist skinheads feel that the United States is headed toward an inevitable race war in which they would be more than willing to fight. The movement is particularly violent, and many experts believe racist skinheads are among the most dangerous of all alt-right groups. Skinhead youths have committed crimes such as racist-inspired vandalism, which includes spray-painting racist slurs and offensive symbols on schools, businesses, and homes. They have also attacked members of the minority groups they hate in crimes ranging from assault to murder. Skinheads who are caught, arrested, and sentenced for their crimes usually join racist skinhead gangs in juvenile correctional facilities and prisons. There they find support in keeping their ideologies alive.

The largest skinhead hate group of the twenty-first century is Blood & Honour. Founded in 1987 in England by singer and white supremacist Ian Stuart Donaldson, it has members across Europe, the United States, and Canada. They are preparing for a race war and see themselves as the "shock troops" (soldiers trained to carry out a sudden attack) for this revolution. Donaldson once said, "Eventually there will be a race war and we have to be strong enough in numbers to win it. I'll die to keep [England] pure and if it means bloodshed at the end of the day, then let it be."

CHRISTIAN IDENTITY GROUPS

The Christian Identity movement believes in the idea of "pure" races. Members believe white people are the true descendants of the fabled Lost Tribes of ancient Israel. The conquering king of Assyria expelled these ten tribes from Israel in 722 BCE, and then they disappeared from the historical record. Christian Identitarians believe whites, as an ancient people, are therefore the chosen race. The movement's followers are racist, anti-Semitic, anti-Muslim, anti-atheist (against people who don't believe in a god or gods), and anti-LGBTQI. Members of this movement also tend to be white nationalists and anti-government—unless the "pure" races with whom they identify run the government. Most Christian Identity groups are small and isolated, and experts think the number of global members is between twenty-five thousand and fifty thousand people. In the United States, they are supported on a national level by organizations such as America's Promise Ministries and Kingdom Identity Ministries, both of which publish and distribute extremist materials. The Christian Identity movement has few supporters among mainstream Christians. The anti-Jewish nature of the Christian Identity movement is in direct conflict with the beliefs of most Christians.

Christian Identity theology (the study and practice of religious faith) includes a belief in millennialism, which says that the world is in its final days. Millennialists believe that humankind is approaching a final battle between good and evil, which they feel will be based on race. In their theology, white people are good, and everyone else is evil. Because they think the end of the world will come soon, most believers in Christian Identity tend to distrust secular (nonreligious) institutions. They hold themselves only to the standards of their religious beliefs.

This apocalyptic (end-of-the-world) vision also leads some followers to isolate themselves from society and organized government. They often live in remote and secluded camps and compounds. The Midwest and Oklahoma are centers of the movement. Some experts view the Christian Identity movement as a religious cult. More extreme members have committed acts of terrorism. For example, members of the Phineas Priesthood carried out a series of bank robberies and bombings in Spokane, Washington, in 1996.

ANTI-SEMITIC GROUPS

Most twenty-first-century anti-Semitic hate groups are extreme right-wing groups—white nationalists, Christian Identity groups, and neo-Nazis such as Vanguard America. Some black separatist groups, such as the Nation of Islam, have been criticized for anti-Semitic leanings. And some Muslim nations and Islamic groups that are fundamentalist (believing in the absolute authority of sacred religious texts and teachings) express animosity toward both Israel and Judaism.

Anti-Semitism can take the form of prejudicial treatment of Jews, such as refusing to allow Jews to join a club or organization. It also

CULTS

In many ways, some hate groups share the characteristics of cults. A cult is a group of people strongly devoted to a person, belief, movement, or work. Many cults are religious in nature, with followers attached to a specific religious leader. In religious cults, the followers worship the leader, who is typically a charismatic individual with an appealing message. Cults discourage individual freedoms and encourage unthinking, unquestioning devotion. They are usually isolated from mainstream society, and leaders make it difficult, often dangerous, for members to reject and leave the cult.

Hate groups that form around charismatic individuals are the most cultlike. This is especially true of hate groups based on a specific religious ideology, such as the Ku Klux Klan, Westboro Baptist Church, and the Christian Identity movement. Strong leaders in these groups can convince followers to adopt the group's beliefs and participate in destructive activities. Hate groups with a broader leadership and that are less connected to religious ideals are less likely to be defined as cults.

can be verbal or physical harassment and outright violence toward individuals or buildings. Anti-Semitic hate crimes decreased in the United States in the first decade of the twenty-first century. However, the election of Donald Trump as president of the United States in 2016 has led to a new surge in anti-Semitism, especially in schools and on college campuses. The Anti-Defamation League reports that anti-Semitic incidents—including physical assaults, vandalism, and attacks on Jewish institutions—increased 57 percent in 2017, Trump's first full year in office.

THE NEO-NAZI MOVEMENT

The neo-Nazi movement admires and promotes the ideology of Adolf Hitler's Nazi Party in 1930s Germany. This includes ideals of white supremacy, white nationalism, and anti-Semitism. Neo-Nazis are usually homophobic and racist. They believe all social problems are rooted in what they claim is a Jewish conspiracy to control the governments, banks, and media outlets of the world. This view is called the Zionist Occupation Government theory. (Zionism is an international movement for the establishment of a Jewish national or religious community in the Middle East. The term is used in the twenty-first century to signal support of modern Israel.)

The largest of the dozens of neo-Nazi groups of the twenty-first century is the National Socialist Movement, with chapters across the United States. This group, founded in 1974 as an offshoot of the American Nazi Party, honors Adolf Hitler, spouts violent anti-Jewish rhetoric, and believes that all but those the group views as purebred heterosexual whites should be deported. Neo-Nazis tend to use many of the symbols of Hitler's Nazi Party, such as the swastika (a geometrical cross at right angles). Some neo-Nazis attend marches and rallies wearing Nazi uniforms, call out the same chants and slogans from the original German party, and give the Nazi salute to their leaders.

Members of the National Socialist Movement in Draketown, Georgia, held a swastika burning after a rally in April 2018. The earlier rally was met with an opposing counterprotest by Draketown community members.

HOLOCAUST DENIERS

Hand in hand with anti-Semitic hate groups are Holocaust deniers. Holocaust deniers insist either that the Holocaust never happened or that the number of victims of this genocide was much lower than reported. Deniers claim that the Holocaust itself was a hoax, part of a Jewish conspiracy to gain sympathy for and advance the interests of Jews at the expense of the white European majority. Holocaust deniers are by definition anti-Semitic, although not all anti-Semites deny the Holocaust.

ANTI-MUSLIM GROUPS

Muslims are victims of religious-based hatred too. Anti-Muslim hate groups direct their hatred toward all followers of Islam, whether in the United States or in other countries. They do not distinguish between mainstream Islam and its extremist offshoots. Members of anti-Muslim hate groups believe that the Islamic faith is by nature violent, intolerant, and sexist. They also believe that Islam is strongly opposed to the Christian values of the United States and to traditional Western values such as individual freedoms. Many mistakenly believe that all Muslims want to overthrow Western democracy and replace it with Sharia, laws that are based on religious principles from the Islamic holy book, the Quran. They believe that all Muslims want to wage jihad (holy war) against the United States and its allies.

Islamophobic groups gained membership immediately after the 9/11 attacks, particularly in the United States. The most extreme anti-Muslim hate groups do not consider Islam a religion. They view it as a totalitarian political ideology (a regime where all aspects of individual life are ruled by the state). They argue that Muslims do not value the freedoms of religion and assembly guaranteed to Americans under the First Amendment to the Constitution.

Many Islamophobic Americans believe, falsely, that Islam is a religion that promotes violence and discrimination. This group of ACT for America protesters holds signs against Sharia, or Islamic law. They believe Sharia is a threat to the United States.

ACT for America, the largest anti-Muslim group in the United States, was founded in 2007. It claims to have more than one thousand chapters and 750,000 members, although the Southern Poverty Law Center believes those numbers are exaggerated. It works to combat the threat members feel Muslims in the United States pose to American democracy. Brigitte Gabriel, head of the group, has said that a practicing Muslim, who believes in the teachings of the Quran, "cannot be a loyal citizen to the United States."

Many anti-Muslim groups want to limit or end immigration into the United States from majority-Muslim countries. They fear that Islamic terrorists may be among immigrants or refugees from these countries and that they may ultimately engineer another attack on the level of the 9/11 attacks. All the same, the only attacks since 9/11 have come from homegrown terrorists. Anti-Muslim groups support the ban on travel from majority-Muslim countries imposed by the Trump administration in 2018.

Anti-Muslim hate groups have committed a variety of hate crimes. They range from bullying and harassing Muslim women wearing head scarves to vandalizing and destroying mosques. The level of violence increased after the 2016 election of Trump as president of the United States. The Council on American-Islamic Relations reports that hate crimes targeting US Muslims increased 15 percent during Trump's first full year in office. Trump and some members of his administration express some of the same basic fears as anti-Muslim groups. They use these opinions to support policies and laws such as the travel ban and other immigration restrictions.

ANTI-IMMIGRANT GROUPS

Anti-immigrant hate groups are opposed to all new immigration to the United States, especially from non-European countries whose populations are not majority white. These hate groups want to halt all immigration as a step toward moving the United States to an all-white majority.

Xenophobia—or fear and hatred of immigrants and other people from other countries—is not new. Historically, Americans have met each new group of immigrants with resistance. For example, many white Americans accused Irish immigrants of the mid-nineteenth century, Chinese immigrants of the late nineteenth century, and Italian immigrants of the early twentieth century of being criminals. They accused them of stealing jobs from other Americans and of not

Anti-immigrant protesters gathered outside a US Border Patrol processing center in Murrieta, California, in July 2014. The activists were rallying against an increase in the number of undocumented immigrant children caught crossing the border between the United States and Mexico.

assimilating (blending) into mainstream society. In the twenty-first century, xenophobia is directed primarily at two groups, Latino and Muslim immigrants.

Anti-immigrant groups such as American Border Patrol and ProEnglish are opposed to Spanish-speaking immigrants, whether they came into the country through legal or illegal means. The groups call for the swift and immediate deportation of all illegal immigrants. Many members advocate violence against legal and illegal immigrants.

In 2016, during Trump's campaign for president of the United States, he talked about extending a border wall between Mexico and the United States. He and his supporters believe that a physical barrier would limit immigrants from Mexico and other nations to the south, the majority of whom enter the United States through Mexico.

THE ALT-RIGHT

The label alt-right (short for alternative right) describes a variety of loosely connected, extreme-right political groups. Richard Spencer, president of the National Policy Institute, a white supremacist think tank based in Arlington, Virginia, coined the term *alt-right*. He came up with the name Alternative Right for an online publication in 2010. Not all alt-right groups have the same prejudices, but the phrase represents people with extreme-right ideologies. They include white supremacists, white nationalists, neo-Nazis, neo-Confederates, and other white identity groups. The term also represents those who hold anti-Semitic, anti-Muslim, anti-immigrant, anti-feminist, and anti-LGBTQI views.

Members of the alt-right tend to have nationalist views, oppose nonwhite immigration, and dislike diversity and inclusion. They make fun of what they view as political correctness—a worldview that avoids forms of expression or action perceived to exclude, marginalize, or insult groups of people who are socially disadvantaged. They also dismiss identity politics, which lays out the shared concerns of people of a given race, gender, religion, or other demographic. Often members of the alt-right use the term *snowflakes* to refer to people who are offended by extreme views and whom they view as fragile and delicate. The alt-right sometimes uses the term *social justice warriors* in a negative way to describe Americans who fight for civil rights and other progressive causes.

Many in the alt-right associate with the European Identitarian movement. Identitarians want to preserve their countries' ethnic and cultural identities. But in their effort to do so, Identitarians often hold deep-seated racist and anti-immigrant ideologies. American alt-right members say they want to preserve the country's white culture. They also claim to support the traditional Christian values of the United States, which they express as intolerance of Muslims, Jews, and members of other non-Christian religions.

Members of the alt-right tend to follow news reporting on far-right websites. Like other Americans, they use Reddit, Twitter, Facebook, and other social media to communicate with one another. High-profile spokespeople of the alt-right, such as former Trump adviser Steve Bannon, are attracting growing numbers of young people who share the same white nationalist beliefs. The alt-right is very visible, but it is an extremist viewpoint and is not in the mainstream of American political thought.

Anti-immigrant hate groups also support the wall, and the idea has gained mainstream support since Trump's election.

Trump, along with members of hate groups and individuals with anti-immigrant leanings, also opposes sanctuary cities. These cities purposely limit cooperation with federal immigration enforcement of policies and laws the cities feel are unjust. They may refuse to charge or detain immigrants for petty charges such as not paying the fare on subways. Or they may deny federal immigration officials space and resources.

The anti-immigration movement is as strong in Europe as it is in the United States. In Europe most of the anger is focused on the large number of immigrants from northern Africa and other Muslim nations. The xenophobia is part of the growing nationalism across the European continent, which is fueling a wave of alt-right politicians seeking to slow or end immigration.

BLACK NATIONALIST GROUPS

Not all hate groups are conservative or politically right wing. Black nationalist groups are on the liberal end of the political spectrum. These groups seek separate economic and cultural development for black individuals of African descent. To become free of racial prejudice and discrimination of white-dominated society, their goal is to create separate white and black nations.

Not all black nationalists practice hate. Some simply want solidarity among black Americans. Others, however, hold strong antiwhite stances and oppose integration and interracial marriage. Some black nationalists are anti-Semitic and anti-LGBTQI. More extreme black nationalists commit acts of violence and terror against white individuals and institutions. For example, Gavin Eugene Long, who shot and killed three police officers and wounded three others in Baton Rouge, Louisiana, in July 2016 was thought to be a member of a black nationalist or separatist group.

The oldest and one of the best-known black separatist groups in US history is the Nation of Islam, led by Louis Farrakhan. Wallace D. Fard and Elijah Muhammad founded the group in Detroit, Michigan, in 1930. Black activist Malcolm X was a member in the 1950s. The Nation of Islam promotes black supremacist, anti-Semitic, and homophobic views. The group is opposed to interracial marriage and other race mixing, which they feel weakens the black race.

Another well-known black separatist group is the New Black Panther Party (also known as the New Black Panther Party for Self Defense). This group shares nothing but a name with the original Black Panther Party. Huey Newton and Bobby Seale formed that

Members of the New Black Panther Party in Los Angeles, California, raise their fists in nonviolent support of an anti-racism rally in 2010. The Southern Poverty Law Center classifies the organization as a hate group, although levels of extremism among the members of the New Black Panther Party varies—as it does in all hate groups.

group in 1966 and promoted armed resistance in response to police brutality against African Americans. The Black Panther Party officially disbanded in 1982.

The New Black Panther Party, which has no formal relationship with the original group, formed in Dallas, Texas, in 1989. It promotes a ten-point platform (set of principles) that includes demands for full employment, decent housing, and the release from prison of all black people in America. This platform reflects very real problems affecting black Americans, including high levels of black unemployment (6.6 percent in July 2018, two-thirds higher than the overall rate of 3.9 percent). Black people have high rates of incarceration, representing 34 percent of the total prison population, but only 18 percent of the general US population. Black Americans also have higher levels of substandard housing—7.5 percent of black Americans live in substandard housing, compared to just 2.8 percent of whites. Although their concerns are rooted in the reality of injustice, this party's tactics categorize them as a hate group. The Anti-Defamation League describes the group as "the largest organized anti-Semitic and racist black militant group in America." In support of their platform, the group's leaders have encouraged violence against whites, Jews, and law enforcement officers.

ANTI-LGBTQI GROUPS

LGBTQI Americans are also the target of hate and violence from organized groups. Citing religion, many of these groups oppose identities outside heterosexual (straight) and binary gender (the system with two genders assigned at birth) norms. Some of the most notorious anti-LGBTQI organizations are churches, typically conservative evangelical churches. (Evangelical faiths believe in salvation through Jesus Christ.) The Westboro Baptist Church of Topeka, Kansas, is among the most prominent. Its members have protested at a high school with an openly gay star football student-athlete and at an event promoting an LGBTQI-themed children's book. Its members have also showed up at military funerals, claiming that God is punishing the United States for tolerating same-sex relationships by killing American soldiers.

Anti-LGBTQI groups are by nature homophobic. They view same-sex relationships as criminal and link LGBTQI identities to a variety of crimes, including pedophilia (sex crimes against children). Groups with a homophobic point of view oppose same-sex marriage and believe that such unions—and LGBTQI people in general—are a threat to the institution of marriage itself. More extreme homophobic viewpoints claim that a global agenda highlighting LGBTQI issues in the media seeks to destroy Christianity.

Most anti-LGBTQI groups affiliate with the Christian Right—a religious sector of evangelical Christian preachers and churches. They often defend their hatred of LGBTQI peoples in terms of "religious freedom" and "religious liberty." They argue that under the Constitution's First Amendment, which guarantees the freedom of religion, they can choose to turn away LGBTQI individuals from their churches. They also feel that businesses run by Christian Right owners have the right to deny services to LGBTQI individuals. And the US Supreme Court has upheld this right in a number of cases, including the 2018 case *Masterpiece Cakeshop, Ltd. v. Colorado Civil Rights Commission*. In this court case, the US Supreme Court upheld the right of the owner of Colorado's Masterpiece Cakeshop to refuse to make a cake for the wedding of a gay couple.

Some anti-LGBTQI groups, such as Mass Resistance, say they want to preserve the traditional nuclear family (a mother, father, and their children). They want to lessen what they view as a strong LGBTQI influence in public schools and other public forums. These groups would like to remove legal protections for LGBTQI individuals, roll back same-sex marriage, and criminalize (or recriminalize) other aspects of LGBTQI relationships and expressions of identity.

NAZI SYMBOLS AND HATE GROUPS

Many right-wing hate groups share the white nationalist views of Nazi Germany. They use Nazi symbols and slogans too. Many white supremacist and neo-Nazi groups ornament their clothing, posters, and websites with the swastika, Iron Cross, and Nazi and fascist slogans.

White supremacists also use a slogan they call the 14 words. David Lane, white supremacist and former KKK member, coined the slogan while he was in prison. (Among other things, he had been found guilty of and sentenced for the murder of Jewish radio host Alan Berg in 1987.) It reads, in fourteen words: "We must secure the existence of our people and a future for White children." White supremacists identify one another with the greeting "14," and the number 14 has become a popular tattoo among white supremacists.

Also popular among white supremacist groups is the numeric code 88. It stands for the eighth letter of the Roman alphabet—*H*. Together, the two *H*'s stand for the German words Heil Hitler (Hail Hitler), a Nazi greeting and salute in praise of Adolf Hitler. Some white supremacists combine the two numbers into the 1488 symbol.

Neo-Nazis and other white supremacist groups often chant the slogans "blood and soil" and "you will not replace us." The first phrase is an Americanized version of *Blut und Boden*, a former Nazi slogan that means "blood and soil." It stands for the belief that ethnic identity is based only on genetics or blood descent (blood) and homeland (soil). "You will not replace us" comes from a French phrase, *le grand replacement*. It refers to large numbers of nonwhite immigrants in France, who French white supremacists believe are replacing white French people as the country's majority race. Neo-Nazis sometimes adapt this chant into "Jews will not replace us" to more specifically fit their beliefs.

MORE ALT-RIGHT SYMBOLS

Some right-wing hate group symbols are religious. They date back to the Crusades of the eleventh, twelfth, and thirteenth centuries, when Christian European armies fought to recapture the Holy Land of the Middle East from Muslim rule. For example, some of the protesters at the 2017 Charlottesville Unite the Right rally carried signs and shields with a red cross emblazoned with the words *deus vult* (Latin for "God wills it"). The red cross is reminiscent of the cross that the Knights Templar (a Roman Catholic military order that fought in the Crusades) wore on their capes and tunics. *Deus vult* was a rallying cry of some Christian knights in the first Crusade of 1101. (Latin was the official language of the Roman Catholic Church until the mid-twentieth century.) By using these symbols, members of the alt-right are connecting to the Islamophobia of the Crusades.

Not all right-wing hate symbols are ancient in origin. The unofficial symbol of the white nationalist movement is a green cartoon frog named Pepe, created by cartoonist Matt Furie in his 2005 comic *Boys Club*. The frog became an inside joke and meme in various mainstream internet forums. Celebrities began using the image, and it became very popular. However, white supremacist supporters of Trump during the 2016 presidential election began to adapt the Pepe meme with swastikas and other racist imagery. After the election, Pepe continues to be linked with alt-right and white nationalist organizations.

Matt Furie, the creator of the green cartoon frog known as Pepe, has condemned the far right movement for adapting his character into a symbol of hate. In this image, a protester in Berkeley, California, holds a sign of Pepe during a protest against the cancellation of a speech by American conservative political commentator Ann Coulter at the University of California, Berkeley, campus in April 2017.

The Anti-Defamation League officially recognizes the cartoon as a hijacked hate symbol.

The league hosts a large online database of symbols used by hate groups across the country. To learn if a symbol or slogan is associated with a hate group, the Hate Symbols Database is a good place to check.

MALE SUPREMACY GROUPS

Male supremacy is an ideology that views women as genetically inferior to men. In their minds, women are on Earth solely to reproduce and provide sexual pleasure to men. They believe men can and should dominate women (violently, if necessary), and that any gains females make in American society are harmful to males.

Male supremacists believe that strong women threaten their own masculinity, take away their jobs, and take their place as the head of the traditional nuclear family. Sometimes male supremacists blame women (and an alleged feminist conspiracy) for various societal problems. They often point to prominent women in politics and female leaders of industry as examples of women who have gone too far beyond a woman's traditional role. Extreme male supremacists support harassing and physically assaulting women to maintain male supremacy.

Some male supremacists call themselves men's rights activists. This is a nod to the second-wave women's rights movement of the 1970s. Although their primary target is frequently women, these men are part of the alt-right universe. Their point of view often goes hand in hand with the same white supremacist, anti-LGBTQI, and anti-immigrant views of alt-right individuals and groups.

The two main male supremacist hate groups in the United States are A Voice for Men and Return of Kings. Houston, Texas-based Paul Elam, a divorced father and men's rights activist, founded A Voice for Men in 2008. The group also has a website, which focuses on what it sees as anti-male bigotry. Members argue that institutionalized feminism has created a world that hates men. As a key example, they point to US courts, which they feel are biased in favor of women. Washington, DC-based Daryush "Roosh" Valizadeh, a self-proclaimed pickup artist (good at attracting sexual partners) and anti-feminist blogger, founded Return of Kings in 2012. This group has advocated for, among other things, the repeal of women's suffrage (the right to vote) and the legalization of rape on private property. Valizadeh later claimed that those thoughts on rape were satire (humorous exaggeration).

ALT-LEFT GROUPS

The majority of US hate groups in the twenty-first century represent far-right, white supremacist views. However, left-wing hate groups—commonly known as the alt-left—have sprung up in response to the rise of alt-right hate groups. Alt-left organizations that actively promote hate and violence are also considered hate groups.

Among the most extreme alt-left groups are anti-fascist groups that oppose the neo-Nazi and neo-fascist movements. These groups, often called antifa (for "anti-fascist") first appeared in

Extreme alt-left members of the antifa movement (*above*) often protest at alt-right rallies. Antifa protesters demonstrated against the Unite the Right rally in Charlottesville, Virginia, in August 2017 and at Unite the Right 2 gatherings in August the following year. They attacked rallygoers with verbal insults as well as physical violence.

Europe immediately before the start of World War II. They formed as a way to fight the spread of fascism—a political system, headed by a dictator, that puts nation and race above the individual and in which the government controls all business and labor. The antifa in the United States launched in Minneapolis-Saint Paul, Minnesota, in the 1980s as a response to a growing neo-Nazi movement there. In the twenty-first century, antifa members often attend neo-Nazi, racist skinhead, and white supremacist events. They typically wear all-black clothing and facial coverings to avoid being identified by the police and to protect themselves from pepper spray. Some antifa use so-called black bloc tactics, which include protesting without a permit.

HATE GROUPS BY NUMBER

CATEGORY	NUMBER OF GROUPS IN UNITED STATES, IN 2017	LARGEST OR MOST NOTABLE
BLACK NATIONALIST	233	Nation of Islam, New Black Panther Party
NEO-NAZI	121	National Socialist Movement, Vanguard America
ANTI-MUSLIM	113	ACT for America, Soldiers of Odin USA
WHITE NATIONALIST	100	Identity Evropa, The Right Stuff
KU KLUX KLAN	72	Ku Klux Klan
RACIST SKINHEAD	71	Blood & Honour, Hammerskins
ANTI-LGBTQI	51	Mass Resistance, Westboro Baptist Church
NEO-CONFEDERATE	31	Identity Dixie, League of the South
ANTI-IMMIGRANT	22	American Border Patrol, ProEnglish
CHRISTIAN IDENTITY	20	America's Promise Ministries, Kingdom Identity Ministries
HATE MUSIC	15	NSM88, Resistance Records
HOLOCAUST DENIAL	10	Committee for Open Debate on the Holocaust, Deir Yassin Remembered
MALE SUPREMACY	2	A Voice for Men, Return of Kings
ALT-RIGHT	1	Ghost
GENERAL HATE	53	American Guard, Proud Boys
ALT-LEFT	Unknown	Antifa, Black Bloc

Most of the hate groups that the Southern Poverty Law Center tracks fall under the general category of the alt-right—white supremacist, white nationalist, neo-Nazi, anti-immigrant, anti-Muslim, and similar groups. The center does not identify or track any alt-left groups, as they have been only loosely defined.

The tactics also involve clashing with alt-right protesters, committing acts of vandalism, and rioting. These actions lead some organizations to define antifa as a hate movement.

Trump popularized the term *alt-left* after the Unite the Right rally in Charlottesville, Virginia, in 2017. In response to a call to condemn the violence there, rather than criticizing the main violence from the alt-right rallygoers Trump claimed violence on both sides, eventually referring to some of the counterprotesters as members of the alt-left. Conservative commentators, such as Sean Hannity on Fox News, have also used the term. Yet not everybody agrees with the categorization of left-wing protesters as alt-left. Oren Segal, director of the Anti-Defamation League's Center on Extremism, claims that the alt-left is a "made-up term" because there is no single organized alt-left movement or distinct alt-left groups. Critics believe that calling left-wing groups or counterprotests "alt-left" is a calculated move to shift criticism away from Trump and the alt-right movement.

CHAPTER 4

ENACTING HATE:
HATE CRIMES

On a late Saturday night, June 25, 2011, a group of young white men and women in the largely white town of Puckett, Mississippi, were having a birthday party for a friend. They were running out of beer, but all the local liquor stores had closed for the night. The friends decided to travel to nearby Jackson, where liquor stores were open later.

Before they left, one of the men, eighteen-year-old Deryl Dedmon Jr., began talking about using the trip to find and attack local blacks. Dedmon started collecting bottles to throw at any black people they saw. He told his friends, "Let's go f**k with some n*****s." They split into two cars, Dedmon's green 1998 Ford F-250 pickup and a white Jeep Cherokee.

The friends drove to a predominantly black area on the west side of Jackson. The group in the Jeep Cherokee passed by a motel and spotted a black man standing near a truck in the parking lot. He had dropped the keys to his truck on the ground and was looking for them. The man was James Anderson, a forty-seven-year-old auto plant worker who lived in Jackson,

Deryl Dedmon Jr. was tried for and found guilty of the June 25, 2011, murder of a black man named James Anderson. Because the murder was inspired by racial hatred, Dedmon's sentence carried an extra penalty as a hate crime.

Mississippi. He was an avid churchgoer and sang tenor in his church choir. He liked to garden, and he and his partner of seventeen years were raising a young relative. The group in the Jeep Cherokee called Dedmon on a cell phone to ask him and the others to join them. The two vehicles pulled into the motel parking lot. The white teenagers leaped out of their vehicles and started to attack Anderson, who was alone. They repeatedly punched him in the head, face, and stomach. They yelled racial slurs and shouted "white power" as they attacked Anderson for several minutes.

After beating and robbing Anderson, the driver and passengers of the Jeep Cherokee got into their vehicle and drove out of the parking lot. Anderson slowly pushed himself off the pavement and tried to stagger away, just as Dedmon started his Ford F-250 and aimed it at him. Dedmon deliberately drove into

Anderson, knocking him to the ground and running over his body. As he left the scene, driving at high speed, Dedmon allegedly told his friends, "I ran that n****r over."

Anderson lay in a pool of blood in the motel parking lot. When he was discovered the next morning, he was taken to a local hospital in critical condition. He died of his injuries a few days later.

Police found and arrested Dedmon on July 6. Partially because of the racial slurs he uttered during the attack, officials considered the crime racially motivated and determined that it was a hate crime. "This was a crime of hate," said Hinds County district attorney Robert Shuler Smith. (Hinds County was the county in which the crime was committed. Smith was the attorney who prosecuted the teens.) "Dedmon murdered this man because he was black."

A few weeks later, the FBI entered the investigation to determine if federal civil rights crimes had occurred. As part of the investigation, FBI agents discovered that Dedmon and his friends were involved in a larger pattern of racially motivated attacks. For several months, they had been harassing and assaulting black people. They threw glass bottles, shot black people with metal ball bearings from a slingshot, and punched and kicked others. The attack on Anderson was just the most recent of many such attacks.

On September 20, 2011, a grand jury indicted (charged) Dedmon on a charge of capital murder (murder for which a guilty defendant could face the death penalty). The jury also indicted him on a federal hate crime charge (a crime motivated by prejudice and hate that holds harsher sentences on a federal level). Several of the other teenagers who were present that night were also indicted on federal hate crime and conspiracy charges.

Dedmon pled guilty to the charges. He was sentenced to two concurrent life sentences (to be served at the same time) in a federal prison. His friends also pled guilty. They were sentenced to between four and fifty years in prison. Dedmon is not eligible for parole.

DEFINING HATE CRIMES

Hate itself is not a crime. Anyone can legally hate whomever they want to hate. Acting on that hate, however, can be a crime. The FBI defines hate crime as "a criminal offense against a person or property motivated in whole or in part by an offender's bias against a race, religion, disability, sexual orientation, ethnicity, gender, or gender identity." A hate crime, then, is a crime inspired by hatred toward or bias against a particular group. The bias can be based on race, ethnicity, religion, country of origin, gender, gender identity, sexual orientation, or a person's disabilities. The intent—the reason—behind the crime determines whether it is a hate crime.

Hate crimes include a wide range of illegal activity, from bullying and harassment to property damage and physical assault. They include threats and intimidation, stalking, hate mail, trespassing, vandalism and property damage, arson, burglary and theft, fraud, aggravated assault or battery, sexual assault, and murder.

The FBI has been investigating hate crimes as far back as World War I. At that time, however, the federal government viewed the protection of civil rights as primarily a local function and did not handle local civil rights crimes. With the passage of the Civil Rights Act in 1964 and the murders of civil rights workers in Mississippi in June 1964, the FBI took an active role in investigating hate crimes. From then on, federal authorities have played a role in investigating hate crimes of particular violence and brutality.

For many years, collecting data about hate crimes was left to state and local authorities. Collection and reporting was spotty, and cross-state comparisons were difficult. Hate crime laws differed from state to state. Some states had less interest than other states do in pursuing and collecting the data. Collecting hate crime data became a federal responsibility in 1991, with the passage of the Hate Crime Statistics Act. This act required the attorney general of the United States to collect data "about crimes that manifest [show] evidence of prejudice based on race, religion, sexual orientation, or ethnicity." This responsibility has since shifted to the FBI, which is now the central resource for all hate crime statistics.

As part of its Hate Crime Statistics Program, the FBI compiles data from 15,254 state and local law enforcement agencies and reports results every year. Hate crime data has become more consistent and more accurate under the FBI's watch, although the bureau still relies on local authorities to provide much of the raw (unanalyzed) data.

HATE CRIMES ON THE RISE

A person in any group can be the target of a hate crime. In the James Anderson case, Deryl Dedmon Jr. and his friends committed the crime because they had a hatred of black people, and Anderson was black. So in addition to the charges of assault and murder, the teens were charged with a hate crime, which carries harsher penalties.

Hate crimes are neither new nor rare. In 2016 (the most recent year for which data is available) the FBI reported 6,121 incidents of hate crime in the United States affecting 7,615 victims. This represents a 5 percent increase over the previous year and a 10 percent increase since 2014. Hate groups and their members can and do commit hate crimes, but the majority of hate crimes are not committed by members of recognized hate groups. Instead, they are committed by individuals who attack other individuals because of a bias against the victim.

Experts believe that the increase in hate crimes may have several causes and represent various trends. First, the 2016 increase coincided with a presidential election that polarized the nation through an increase in hateful political speech. Much of this political rhetoric demonized nonwhite groups and Muslims. The hateful speech corresponded to an increase in crimes against various minority groups, especially African Americans, Muslims, and Latino immigrants. Anti-Muslim violence in particular increased significantly, more than doubling over the two-year period from 2014 to 2016. Additional research by the Council on

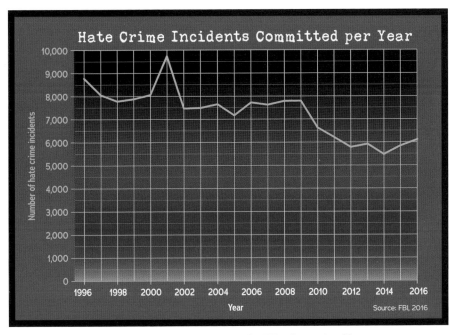

Hate Crime Incidents Committed per Year

Number of hate crime incidents

Year

Source: FBI, 2016

As part of its Hate Crimes Statistic Program, the FBI relies on local law enforcement agencies to report hate crimes that take place in their regions. The number of reporting agencies varies every year, accounting for some margin of error in the statistics. However, the overall trend shows an upswing in hate crimes in the United States since 2014 after several years of a decrease in hate crimes.

American-Islamic Relations indicates further increases in anti-Muslim hate crime in 2017. Second, the numbers may reflect that the FBI is getting better at tracking hate crime data. The bureau is focusing more attention on this issue than it did in the early part of the century. So more recent data may be more accurate than older data.

According to the FBI's 2016 data, roughly two-thirds (65 percent) of hate crimes were crimes against people. One-third (34 percent) of hate crimes were against property. The property crimes typically involved vandalism or arson against buildings or other property owned or used by an individual or organization of a target group. These included religious houses of worship such as Jewish synagogues and Islamic mosques.

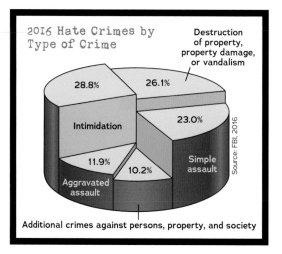

2016 Hate Crimes by Type of Crime

28.8% Intimidation

26.1% Destruction of property, property damage, or vandalism

23.0% Simple assault

11.9% Aggravated assault

10.2% Additional crimes against persons, property, and society

Source: FBI, 2016

This infographic shows the range of hate crimes committed in the United States in 2016. More than two-thirds of the hate crimes were committed against people rather than property.

The FBI further broke down these statistics by the following types of crime:

- intimidation: 28.8 percent
- destruction of property, property damage, or vandalism: 26.1 percent
- simple assault: 23.0 percent
- aggravated assault: 11.9 percent
- additional crimes against persons, property, and society: 10.2 percent

What motivated these hate crimes? The FBI analyzed the data and found the following explanations:

- race/ethnicity/ancestry bias: 57.5 percent
- religious bias: 21.0 percent
- sexual-orientation bias: 17.7 percent
- gender-identity bias: 2.0 percent
- disability bias: 1.2 percent
- gender bias: 0.5

The majority of hate crimes were motivated by prejudice against a person's race, ethnicity, or ancestry. Of those crimes, half (50.2 percent) were directed toward blacks. Another 20.7 percent of these crimes

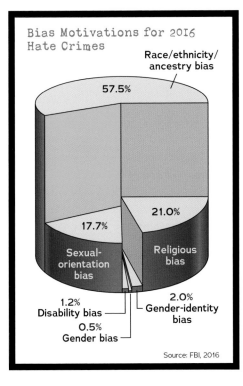

Bias Motivations for 2016 Hate Crimes

Race/ethnicity/ancestry bias — 57.5%

Religious bias — 21.0%

Sexual-orientation bias — 17.7%

Gender-identity bias — 2.0%

Disability bias — 1.2%

Gender bias — 0.5%

Source: FBI, 2016

More than half of the hate crimes committed in the United States in 2016, the most recent year for which data was available, were committed due to bias against a person's race, ethnicity, or ancestry.

involved antiwhite bias, and 10.6 percent involved anti-Hispanic (those from Spanish-speaking origins) or Latino (those of Latin American ancestry) bias, which were usually carried out by white individuals. About 3.8 percent of these crimes had an anti-American Indian or Alaska Native bias. This is a significant percentage since less than 2 percent of the total US population falls into this group. The rest of the crimes were motivated by anti-multiracial bias, anti-Asian bias, anti-Arab bias, and anti-Native Hawaiian or other Pacific Islander bias.

Religious bias drove about one-fifth of reported hate crimes. A little over half (54 percent) of those incidents involved anti-Semitic crimes against individuals or synagogues. Anti-Muslim crimes make up 24.8 percent of total religiously motivated crimes. Experts suggest they are likely the result of continuing prejudice against Muslims post-9/11.

Crimes motivated by bias against a person's sexual orientation targeted mostly gay males, accounting for 62.8 percent of those hate crimes. Transgender individuals are the people most often targeted by people holding gender-identity bias.

ANTI-AMERICAN-INDIAN HATE CRIMES

In May 2017, twenty-year-old Jimmy Smith-Kramer, a member of the Quinault Indian Nation, was celebrating his birthday with friends at a campsite. During the celebration in Grays Harbor County in Washington State, a thirty-two-year-old white man named James Walker drove his pickup truck into the group of young people. He floored the gas pedal into the group, backed up, and then drove forward again, crushing Smith-Kramer and one of his friends. Witnesses claim the driver screamed racial slurs when he ran over the two men. Smith-Kramer, a father of two, died from his injuries.

Of about six thousand hate crime incidents the FBI recorded in 2016, 3.8 percent were against American Indians and Alaska Natives. A 2017 study conducted for National Public Radio and two other institutions found that 35 percent of American Indians have personally experienced racial or ethnic slurs.

American Indians and Alaska Natives have long been the victims of prejudice and hatred in the Americas. Early white settlers and the US army targeted American Indians for extermination. The genocidal violence against and mistreatment of indigenous (native) peoples continued over time to include the violent removal of entire tribes to reservations. It also included forced assimilation of American Indian children through placement in white-run boarding schools. The children couldn't live with their families, speak their own languages, or wear traditional clothing. Because of this legacy, American Indians in the twenty-first century have higher levels of unemployment with a jobless rate of 10 percent in 2017 compared to the national average of 4 percent. They also experience higher levels of poverty than other marginalized groups. Just over one-quarter of the population (25 percent) of American Indian and Alaska Natives in 2017 lived below the poverty line. American Indian women are also at much higher risk for rape and sexual assault. Organized hate groups that specifically target American Indians do not exist. However, American Indians are at high risk of hate crime victimization.

LAWS AGAINST HATE CRIMES

Hate crime legislation in the United States is relatively recent. Throughout the eighteenth, nineteenth, and early twentieth centuries, the country did not have local or federal legislation that directly addressed hate crimes or their victims. If a person or place was the victim of a biased attack, the legal system had no special category for or way of dealing with the motivation behind the crime.

That changed in 1968 when President Lyndon B. Johnson signed the Fair Housing Act of 1968 into law. The law addressed discrimination in housing. Among the act's many provisions is one that makes it illegal to interfere with a person's right to housing because of race, religion, or gender. It specifically outlaws anyone who "by force

President Lyndon B. Johnson signed the Fair Housing Act into law in 1968 as a follow-up to the Civil Rights Act of 1964. Associate Justice Thurgood Marshall *(far right)*, the first black justice of the US Supreme Court, stands next to Minnesota senator Walter Mondale, the chief sponsor of the bill. Many historians mark this legislation as the final large-scale achievement of the civil rights era.

or threat of force willfully injures, intimidates or interferes with or attempts to injure, intimidate or interfere with . . . any person because of his race, color, religion, sex, handicap . . . or national origin."

Only a few crimes, such as tax evasion, mail fraud, and kidnapping, are federal crimes. All other crimes are defined by state and local statutes (laws). States lagged behind the US government in passing laws to deal with hate crimes. In 1978 California became the first state to pass specific hate crime legislation. It allowed for stiffer penalties for murder when "the victim was intentionally killed because of his or her race, color, religion, nationality, or country of origin." In the twenty-first century, forty-five states and the District of Columbia have statutes that criminalize certain types of hate crimes. Only South Carolina, Georgia, Arkansas, Wyoming, and Indiana do not.

Prior to these hate crime laws, the guilty person was charged only with the crime. Hate crime legislation allows prosecutors (the person who brings a legal case to court against someone accused of committing a crime) to seek additional penalties. So most hate crime laws are technically penalty-enhancement statutes. They increase the penalty for the offense because of the added layer of hate.

The additional penalties for committing a hate crime vary from state to state and according to the type of crime. Additional penalties for hate crimes without bodily injury (physical injury) range from a fine to a prison term of up to one year. If the crime involves bodily injury or the use of a firearm, explosives, or fire, the guilty person may be sentenced to a prison term of up to ten years. If the hate crime involves sexual assault, kidnapping, or murder, the punishment can range up to life in prison or, in certain capital offenses, the death penalty. On the federal level, hate crimes involving bias-motivated violence are punishable by ten years to life in prison. Some specific crimes carry the death penalty.

Why the harsher penalties for hate crimes? In the United States, most crimes target an individual victim. But hate crimes are a threat to an entire segment of the population. A mugger who holds up a random person on the street does it for money, without the background or identity of the victim in mind. By contrast, a person who commits a hate crime targets an individual based specifically on race, gender, sexual orientation, or other group characteristics. This poses an active and ongoing threat to other people who fall in the same demographic. So the increased penalties are meant to deter people from committing bias-based crimes. Not all experts believe the penalties have that outcome. But most feel the additional penalty is an important sign of a society's unwillingness to accept hate crime.

In 2009 President Barack Obama signed into law the Matthew Shepard and James Byrd, Jr. Hate Crimes Prevention Act. The new law expanded laws about hate crimes to include a victim's actual or perceived gender, sexual orientation, gender identity, or disability. It was passed in response to the violent deaths of Matthew Shepard, a young gay man murdered in Wyoming by two young homophobic males, and James Byrd Jr., a middle-aged black man murdered in Texas by three white supremacists. Both crimes were so horrific they rose to national attention. In Shepard's case, the young men lured him into the countryside and beat, pistol-whipped, and tortured him before tying him to a fence, where they assumed he would die. He later died at a hospital from head injuries. Byrd's murderers drove him to a remote location where they beat him and urinated on him. With log chains, they tied his ankles to the back of their pickup truck and dragged him until he died. His body was completely dismembered. The Hate Crimes Prevention Act makes it illegal to willfully cause or attempt to cause bodily injury with a firearm, fire, or other dangerous weapon when the crime is committed because of the race, color, religion, or national origin of the victim. The law was also the first federal legislation to expand coverage to include the gender, gender identity, sexual orientation, or disability of the victim.

ANTI-MUSLIM HATE CRIMES IN THE TRUMP ERA

Trump's road to the presidency has been accompanied by a rise of hate crimes of all sorts. Experts point in particular to a rise in hate crimes against Muslims. Gadeir Abbas, an attorney for the Council on American-Islamic Relations, explains this increase by pointing to the many inflammatory statements against Muslims that Trump makes in tweets and speeches. "There has been nothing like this ever, for the Muslim community to be regularly the punching bag of the president of the United States," Abbas says. In 2016, before Trump was elected president, reported hate crimes against American Muslims was at 260. In the year following Trump's election, that number rose to 300. Some of those crimes were particularly violent.

On May 26, 2017, in Portland, Oregon, a drunk man on the Green Line commuter train began shouting at two teenage girls, one wearing a hijab, a traditional Muslim headdress. He yelled insults and taunts, including "Get the f**k out," "Go home, we need Americans here!" "F**k Saudi Arabia!'" and "Free speech or die!"

Three passengers in the train car tried to intervene. In response, the drunk man, identified later as Jeremy Joseph Christian, shouted "Oh, do something b***h!" He pulled out a knife and started to stab the men confronting him. Two of them died at the scene, and a third was seriously wounded. Christian exited the train, and local police arrested him.

Christian was charged with nine criminal charges, including two counts of aggravated murder. The FBI consulted with local authorities about filing possible hate crime charges. Portland's mayor condemned the incident, as did Oregon senator Jeff Merkley. Trump tweeted a reply to the attack from the official presidential account two days later, saying, "The violent attacks in Portland on Friday are unacceptable. The victims were standing up to hate and intolerance. Our prayers are [with] them."

The city of Portland, Oregon, responded to a fatal hate-based stabbing on a commuter train with an outpouring of love and support for the victims. Residents set up a memorial at the Hollywood Transit Center where the train came to a stop after the attack on May 26, 2017.

PROSECUTING HATE CRIMES

If law enforcement officials believe that a crime was inspired by hatred or prejudice, they can ask the prosecutor to add hate crime charges to the other charges the perpetrator will face. The prosecutor will then argue for the conviction of the perpetrator on hate crime charges.

On a local level, hate crime charges allow the prosecution team to ask for higher penalties—usually a longer prison sentence. However, raising the stakes can sometimes make it more difficult for the prosecution to win a conviction. Juries may be reluctant to convict knowing that the person would face more severe punishment with a guilty verdict.

If a hate crime is also covered by federal laws, the local prosecutor and law enforcement will work with the FBI to include federal hate crime charges to the local criminal charges. (Federal crimes include those based on a victim's race, religion, ethnicity, nationality, gender, sexual orientation, gender identity, and disability.) Prosecution of the federal charges typically takes place in a separate trial from the one for the local charges. Local authorities and the FBI decide if the federal charges are in addition to or in place of local hate crime charges. Federal charges carry extra penalties, so if a person is convicted in local and federal courts, the penalty can be significant.

To successfully convict someone of a hate crime, prosecutors must prove that the defendant (the person charged with a crime) committed the crime. They must also prove that hate was the motive behind the crime. This can be very difficult, so prosecuting attorneys look to show a person's outward demonstrations of hate as evidence to prove the motive of hatred. This can be that a person has used prejudicial language, displays hate symbols, admits to prejudice, or has a history of similar bias-inspired acts.

Because the motive behind a hate crime is so difficult to prove, many prosecutors may be reluctant to bring hate crime charges. They may prefer to focus on easier-to-prove traditional criminal charges. The

HATE CRIMES AND DOMESTIC TERRORISM

Some people believe that hate crimes—especially those targeting large groups of people—are acts of terrorism. These crimes, such as the Unite the Right rally attack that killed Heather Heyer and Dylann Roof's mass shooting at the Emanuel African Methodist Episcopal Church in Charleston, frighten huge numbers of the population. But US courts and the legal system view terrorism and hate crimes as two distinct criminal activities.

Hate crimes are inspired by bias or prejudice against a person in a specific social group, such as gay or black people. Terrorism is slightly different. The FBI defines domestic (US) terrorism as acts carried out "by individuals and/or groups inspired by or associated with primarily US-based movements that espouse [believe in] extremist ideologies of a political, religious, social, racial or environmental nature." So hate crimes are committed *against* a person or people of a hated group, while terrorism is committed *in support* of a group's cause. Hate crime has a specific target, and the crime is meant to harm a person belonging to a specific social group. The target is based on the perpetrator's prejudice against that person. But terrorist acts are committed against society in general.

Some experts want authorities to start classifying at least some hate crimes as domestic terrorism. Terrorism charges are often easier to prove than hate crime charges. And because hate crimes are meant to terrorize a given group of people, some experts say they fall under existing terrorism laws.

In addition, states and the US government have more money, people, and other resources to handle terrorism than they do for hate crimes. So if hate crimes were tried as terrorism, prosecutors would perhaps have more success in convicting perpetrators. For the time being, however, authorities draw a clear distinction between hate crimes and terrorism.

Transactional Records Access Clearinghouse at Syracuse University in New York analyzed data from the US Department of Justice from January 2010 to August 2015. The clearinghouse found that federal prosecutors pursued only 13 percent of possible hate crime cases. Only 11 percent of those prosecutions led to a conviction by jury.

The same analysis looked into the reasons federal prosecutors decline to try cases as hate crimes. The most common reason was insufficient evidence (in 21 percent of cases), followed by lack of evidence of criminal intent (17 percent). Weak or insufficient admissible evidence (evidence that a court will not allow because it is biased or wasn't obtained according to law) accounted for another 17 percent of cases. Altogether, concern about the strength of evidence about the motivation behind the crime was the reason for more than half of all decisions not to prosecute.

Reluctance to prosecute hate crimes weakens the effectiveness of hate crime laws. It also seriously skews the collection of accurate hate crime data. If a prosecutor decides not to pursue hate crime charges, even if it is likely a hate crime, authorities will not track that crime as a hate crime.

CHAPTER 5

PROMOTING HATE:
HATE SPEECH

The Westboro Baptist Church in Topeka, Kansas, is a small church, with only about forty members. The church building is a nondescript white house on a corner lot in a quiet residential neighborhood. Fred Phelps founded the church in 1955 and was its lead pastor until his death in 2014. Phelps hated gay and lesbian people with a passion. Many evangelicals like Phelps believe that the Bible prohibits homosexuality, quoting Leviticus 18:22, "You shall not lie with a male as with a woman; it is an abomination."

Phelps went further, claiming that just about every tragedy in the world has been caused by or linked to LGBTQI peoples. For example, he believed that the September 11 terrorist attacks were God's response to the acceptance of homosexuals in the United States. Five years after those attacks, Phelps posted a video in which he said that "the deadly events of 9/11 were direct outpourings of divine retribution [God's punishment], the immediate visitation of God's wrath and vengeance and punishment for America's horrendous sodomite [gay or lesbian]

Twenty-year-old Megan Phelps-Roper and other members of Westboro Baptist Church picket the funeral of a soldier outside Arlington National Cemetery in Arlington, Virginia. Arlington is one of the nation's most prestigious cemeteries for US veterans and service members. (IEDs stands for "improvised explosive devices," or the small, deadly bombs common in war zones of the Middle East in the twenty-first century.)

sins, that worse and more of it was on the way. . . . God is no longer with America, but is now America's enemy. God himself is now America's terrorist."

Phelps preached hate to anyone who would listen, especially the members of his congregation, most of whom were members of his extended family. Anti-LGBTQI hatred is a key part of his church's message. It's in the church's slogan—"God Hates F*gs"—and in the URL of the church website.

The members of the church are activists. Almost every day, someone from the church is protesting in the Topeka area. They protest government offices, local businesses, and other churches that they believe are false prophets (people who rebel against God) because they do not harshly condemn gays and lesbians. They hold up signs that say, "Sodomy is a Crime" and "USA = F*g Nation." The Southern Poverty Law Center tracks Westboro protests and says its church members have picketed at more than forty thousand events since the church first started doing so in 1991.

The church members are best known for protesting at funerals. For example, members of the church picketed the 1998 funeral of Matthew Shepard, the victim of an antigay hate crime in Wyoming. They later picketed the funerals of the victims of the 2012 mass shooting at the Sandy Hook Elementary School in Newtown, Connecticut, where twenty children and six adults were killed. Westboro Baptist Church members argued that the deaths were God's punishment for the acceptance of LGBTQI individuals in society. They also picketed the funerals of the victims of the 2016 mass shooting at the Pulse gay nightclub in Orlando, Florida, celebrating the murders of the club's patrons.

Members of the church have picketed the funerals of thousands of US soldiers killed in combat. They claim that their deaths were punishment for the US government's tolerance and support of LGBTQI rights. For example, on March 10, 2006, seven members of the church flew to Westminster, Maryland, to picket the funeral of twenty-year-old Lance Corporal Matthew Snyder, who had been killed in action in Iraq the week before. Many Americans found the protest extremely disturbing. Albert Snyder, the corporal's father, told a *Time* magazine interviewer that "to me, what they did was just as bad, if not worse, than if they had taken a gun and shot me. At least the wound would have healed."

Snyder was so upset by the church's protest that he sued the church for defamation, intrusion against seclusion (that is, intruding on a private funeral), publicity given to private life, intentional infliction of emotional distress, and civil conspiracy. (Civil conspiracy describes two or more people who make an agreement to act together with the intent to accomplish an unlawful goal with the purpose of harming another.) During the trial, Snyder described his emotional injuries, including tears, anger, and nausea to the point of vomiting. In their defense, lawyers for the church noted that the protesters had followed all local regulations and police instructions. They had even set up their pickets 1,000 feet (305 m) from the site of the funeral, as required by law.

The case was presented to the jury as a family's right to a private funeral versus a church's right to free speech. On October 31, 2007, the jury ruled against the church on most of the charges. The judge awarded Snyder $5 million in damages. The church appealed the verdict, stressing the right to free speech. On March 20, 2010, the appeals court reversed the original verdict and set aside the $5 million judgment.

Snyder then appealed that decision before the US Supreme Court. On March 2, 2011, in a landmark 8–1 ruling, the court upheld the appeals court verdict. In the case—*Snyder v. Phelps*—the court affirmed the church's right to picket Corporal Snyder's funeral. In his majority opinion, Chief Justice John Roberts stated that "what Westboro said, in the whole context of how and where it chose to say it, is entitled to 'special protection' under the First Amendment and that protection cannot be overcome by a jury finding that the picketing was outrageous." So hate speech—no matter how "outrageous"—is protected by the First Amendment of the US Constitution.

The Westboro Baptist Church continues to picket military and other funerals.

WHAT IS HATE SPEECH?

US law has no official definition of hate speech. Some free speech advocates argue that hate speech is too subjective and vague to define. Yet most experts agree in broad terms to a definition of hate speech. Merriam-Webster's legal dictionary defines *hate speech* as "speech that is intended to insult, offend, or intimidate a person because of some trait (race, religion, sexual orientation, national origin, or disability)."

Hate speech is not a crime in the United States. In fact, hate speech is just one of many kinds of speech protected by the First Amendment to the Constitution, even though it is motivated by bias and prejudice. In the United States, hate speech only becomes criminal when it crosses the line to include illegal actions. For example, yelling a racist slogan in public is legal. Spray-painting that same slogan on the side of a building is illegal. It defaces (ruins) property, which is a crime. Calling someone by a racist slur is legal. Physically attacking that person while calling them that same name is illegal because the attack causes physical harm. Writing a racist note is legal. Attaching that note to a rock and throwing it through a window is illegal.

HATE SPEECH AND THE FIRST AMENDMENT

Hate speech, as with most types of speech, is protected under the First Amendment of the US Constitution. The United States was founded partly to ensure "life, liberty, and the pursuit of happiness." This implies a range of individual freedoms, including freedom of speech and expression. The great minds of the time stressed the importance of free speech. Inventor and statesman Benjamin Franklin wrote that "without Freedom of thought, there can be no such Thing as Wisdom; and no such thing as public Liberty, without Freedom of speech."

George Washington, the first president of the United States, said, "For if Men are to be [prevented] from offering their Sentiments on a matter, which may involve the most serious and alarming consequences, that can invite the consideration of Mankind, reason is of no use to us; the freedom of Speech may be taken away, and, dumb and silent we may be led, like sheep, to the Slaughter."

The First Amendment is concise and direct in its protections, and US courts have upheld the First Amendment and freedom of speech through various cases. For example, in 1969 the US Supreme Court heard *Brandenburg v. Ohio*. Clarence Brandenburg, a KKK leader, made racist remarks during a Klan rally in Hamilton County, Ohio, including "Send the Jews back to Israel" and "Bury the n*****s." He was arrested. A lower court convicted him of violating an Ohio law against advocating "crime, sabotage, violence or unlawful methods of terrorism as a means of accomplishing industrial or political reform." Brandenburg appealed his conviction all the way to the US Supreme Court. The court struck down the Ohio law on the grounds that it violated the Klan leader's right to free speech.

The court held that "the constitutional guarantees of free speech and free press do not permit a State to forbid or proscribe [promote] advocacy of the use of force or of law violation except where such advocacy is directed to inciting or producing imminent [immediate] lawless action and is likely to incite or produce such action." So hate speech is allowed as free speech unless and until it encourages illegal actions.

HATE SPEECH ONLINE

Hate speech has flourished on the internet, especially across social media. The major social networks have rules that forbid offensive language, harassment, and cyberbullying. They also use algorithms to try to prevent such postings. Even so, people continue to successfully post content that inflames, threatens, and trolls (deliberately makes controversial comments).

Online behavior, especially when it is anonymous, can be very different from the behavior of individuals in person. A 2014 University of Houston study found that people tend to post more offensive comments when they don't have to reveal their identities. This is called the online disinhibition effect, which says when a person's identity is hidden, that person will believe there are no consequences to what they say. The anonymity leads them to say things they would never say in a face-to-face conversation. The study analyzed online anonymity in the comments sections of online newspapers. It found that 53 percent of anonymous comments included language that was vulgar, racist, profane, or hateful. Only 29 percent of nonanonymous comments were found to be uncivil in this manner. As Walter Isaacson, former editor of *Time* and former chief executive officer of CNN, said, "Internet anonymity is one of many reasons that civility has been drained from our public dialogue."

The 2016 presidential election saw a further erosion of online civility through an eruption of hate speech on the internet. This hate speech most often attacked a specific political candidate or their supporters, sometimes threatening physical violence. It also targeted minorities. The Anti-Defamation League found that from August 1, 2015, through July 31, 2016, more than 2.6 million tweets included anti-Semitic language. Often journalists were targets of those tweets. Of more than eight hundred journalists who received anti-Semitic tweets, the top ten most targeted individuals (all of whom are Jewish) received 83 percent of the offensive tweets. Anti-Muslim online speech was also on the rise. The Southern Poverty Law Center found that between November 8, 2016, and December 8, 2016, more than 1,750 individual anti-Muslim photos and memes were distributed online.

Because of the explosion of online hate, many Americans are calling for new regulations on social media to crack down on hate speech, fake news, and other offensive or misleading content. Others point to the slippery slope issue. That is, regulating speech that most people would find offensive can very quickly lead to regulating other types of speech. Some people worry that this might eventually lead to regulating any speech that offends the government or other people in power. Scholars of free speech point out that the First Amendment protects *all* speech, without regard to type of speech or viewpoint. Unless the speech itself clearly leads to violence, that speech is protected. Any attempts to whittle down those protections, even for hateful speech, could have serious consequences down the road.

WHEN IS HATE SPEECH ILLEGAL?

Several types of speech do not fall under First Amendment protections. In particular, courts have found that the First Amendment does not protect these categories of speech:

- obscenity, as defined by local community standards, whether in text, images, or film
- child pornography, including text, images, or films depicting sexually explicit activities involving a child
- perjury, or willfully lying in court
- blackmail, the action of demanding money from a person in return for not revealing compromising or harmful information about that person
- false speech that is likely to cause harm to others, such as shouting "Fire!" in a crowded theater where a fire is not actually occurring
- true threats, or threatening real violence upon a person
- *fighting words*, meaning "written or spoken words that encourage violence or hatred toward a specific target"
- inciting (encouraging) others to commit violence or criminal acts (including suicide)

HATE SPEECH BEYOND WORDS

Hate speech can take a variety of forms and still be protected by the First Amendment. Over the years, various court rulings have determined that the First Amendment protects anonymous speech, political speech, religious speech, speech critical of the government, and hate speech. Also covered as speech under First Amendment rights are public protests and distribution of traditional and modern media, including newspapers, magazines, books, plays, and video games. The groundbreaking 2010 *Citizens United v. Federal Election Commission* Supreme Court decision also found that monetary contributions to political campaigns, including those made by corporations or unions, are protected by First Amendment rights.

INTERNATIONAL REGULATION OF SPEECH

Different countries have different views about regulating hate speech. Hate speech in the United States falls under the protection of the First Amendment. But protections for every type of speech do not exist in the founding documents of most other countries. Many countries have passed laws to regulate hate speech.

As early as 1881 in France, the Press Law made it illegal to incite racial discrimination, hatred, or violence on the basis of a person's origin or membership in an ethnic, national, racial, or religious group. After World War II, many European countries followed suit and passed regulations on hateful speech, particularly speech from known hate groups. These laws were intended to protect against the type of anti-Semitic, racist, and xenophobic propaganda that had led to World War II. They were also passed to ensure that the Nazi Party and people who supported Nazi ideology did not rise to power again. In Denmark, for example, it is a crime for an individual to make "statements . . . by which a group of persons is threatened, derided [ridiculed] or degraded because of their race, color of skin, national or ethnic background, faith or sexual orientation." Since 1986 the United Kingdom has prohibited racial hatred, in the form of threatening behavior and written material, based on color, race, ethnic origin, and nationality. The law has since expanded protections to include protection against religious hatred and hatred on the grounds of sexual orientation.

Germany outlaws hate speech in general and has expanded its laws to cover hate speech online. Starting January 1, 2018, Germany began enforcing a law specifically requiring social media sites to quickly remove hate speech, fake news, and illegal material such as intentionally false and inflammatory stories and images of the swastika. The new laws have inspired other European countries. France and the United Kingdom are among the countries that have debated or passed similar regulations.

Prohibitions of hate speech exist in other areas of the world as well. In South Africa, for example, hate speech is specifically excluded from the free speech protections included in the nation's constitution. That country is also considering a new Prevention and Combating of Hate Crimes and Hate Speech

When he was Germany's justice minister, Heiko Maas spearheaded the law to remove hate speech from German social media. The law went into effect in 2018.

Bill that would provide even more restrictions on hate speech. Many South Africans support action against hate crimes. But members of the public and critics alike claim that if this bill becomes law, a person could face jail time by simply insulting or ridiculing someone rather than for truly attacking a person for their race, gender, religion, or occupation. These critics fear that South Africans would face an extreme limit to citizens' freedom of expression.

Another argument against broad restrictions on hate speech is that government leaders could potentially use them to put down dissent. Some argue this has been the case for teen blogger Amos Yee in Singapore. Singapore's Maintenance of Religious Harmony Act of 1990 criminalizes hate speech based on race or religion. Some say, in reality, the government has used this law to suppress political and anti-government speech such as Yee's online posts and videos. The teen was convicted in 2015 and sentenced to imprisonment for a post that included an image of Singapore's former prime minister Lee Kuan Yew in a sex act with Margaret Thatcher, a former prime minister of the United Kingdom. Yee was sentenced again for posting a video with language deemed offensive to Christians.

Hate speech can take a variety of forms and still fall under First Amendment protection. Holding a protest, displaying a flag or symbol, or posting on Facebook or Twitter are all viewed as expressing a point of view and are therefore protected as free speech in the United States. An important, historic example of public protest as free speech was the Skokie incident. In 1977 about thirty members of the neo-Nazi National Socialist Party of America wanted to hold a rally and march in the Chicago suburb of Skokie, Illinois. The group was planning to wear Nazi uniforms and carry its flag, which bears an image of the Nazi swastika. The group intentionally chose Skokie because it is home to many Jewish people who had been terrorized by Nazis or survived the Holocaust. The suburb and its residents opposed the march and filed suit to stop the demonstration. The Circuit Court of Cook County, Illinois, allowed the group to march but prohibited the marchers from wearing Nazi uniforms and displaying Nazi swastikas. The circuit court said those actions would be offensive to the Jewish residents of Skokie. The neo-Nazi group challenged the ruling with the support of the American Civil Liberties Union (ACLU), a nonpartisan organization that defends individual freedoms granted by the US Constitution. They argued that the town was restricting the National Socialist Party of America's First Amendment free speech rights. The case eventually made its way to the US Supreme Court, which agreed with the First Amendment arguments and ruled against the town. The court said that even though the people of Skokie would find the demonstration offensive, the group still had the right to march and express its opinions. In the end, the march never took place in Skokie. Instead, the National Socialist Party of America held a rally in downtown Chicago.

A more recent example of public protest as free speech took place in Gainesville, Florida, at the University of Florida. Controversial white nationalist Richard Spencer requested a permit for his group, the National Policy Institute, to hold a protest on the campus on September 12, 2017. The university cited the potential for violence following the

In October 2017, a crowd at the University of Florida in Gainesville protested white nationalist Richard Spencer (*onstage*), who was on campus to give a speech. They marched outside the auditorium while other protesters inside chanted and booed as the white nationalist began his talk.

violence at the Unite the Right rally in Charlottesville, Virginia, and denied the request. The ACLU came to Spencer's defense, declaring that his right to free speech should not be denied because of the potential bad behavior of others. "The fact that other people have advocated for violence or have engaged in acts of violence can never be the . . . [basis] by which freedom of speech can be curtailed [limited] or restrained," said Michael Barfield, vice president of the ACLU of Florida. Spencer and the ACLU won. The event was rescheduled for October and met with counterprotesters, as was their First Amendment right.

HATE SPEECH ON THE INTERNET

Before the internet, extremists promoted their causes and recruited new members by printing copies of their manifestos (group aims), passing out leaflets on street corners, and holding meetings in basements or old storefronts. In the twenty-first century, most hate speech is shared and spread online through posts on social media such as Twitter, Facebook, and Instagram. Because of the reach of social media, a hateful message or meme can travel around the globe instantly. It can go viral in just hours.

Facebook and Twitter are the most popular media for sharing hate speech. But hate speech also shows up in photos on Instagram and videos on YouTube. Reddit and 4chan are also popular platforms for hate-fueled online conversations. And most organized hate groups have their own websites and social media accounts. They encourage followers to share links, articles, and posts.

Some social networks are devoted to free expression of all types, including hate speech. Gab, for example, is a microblogging service, similar to Twitter. It allows all kinds of speech on its site and bills itself as "The Free Speech Social Network." It does not censor posts in any way. The site describes itself as, "an ad-free social network dedicated to preserving individual liberty, the freedom of speech, and the free flow of information on the internet. A free and open internet is essential to the future of a free world."

Many mainstream social media outlets are trying to identify and remove hate speech from their networks. Each site does it differently, but most start with clear rules for users. Facebook, for example, has created a set of community standards that it believes encourages respectful behavior, specifically addressing hate speech. The company policy reads, in part, "We do not allow hate speech on Facebook because it creates an environment of intimidation and exclusion and in some cases may promote real-world violence." Facebook categorizes hate speech as an attack against people based on protected characteristics that include "race, ethnicity, national origin, religious affiliation, sexual orientation, caste, sex, gender, gender identity, and serious disease or disability." Facebook also expands some protections to include immigration status.

Twitter restricts hateful images and hateful names in user profiles. Its policies also clearly address hateful content on its site, saying, "You may not promote violence against or directly attack or threaten other people on the basis of race, ethnicity, national origin, sexual orientation, gender, gender identity, religious affiliation, age, disability, or serious disease."

Facebook, Twitter, and similar sites use algorithms and automated software to search the sites for messages with hateful speech. They also rely on other users (and nonusers) to monitor, identify, and report offensive posts. When these users report content that violates rules and policies, the site will take down the offending posts.

Internet service providers can refuse to host accounts or servers that send hateful messages across their services. If an organization or individual breaks a service provider's content rules, the provider can refuse to do business with them. In this way, many hate groups have found it difficult to find businesses that will host their websites. They use smaller, more obscure providers. These offensive sites may also have trouble registering web domain names. So they go onto the deep web, a secretive part of the internet that is accessible only with certain software. Or they may go onto the dark web—a part of the deep web that also hides a user's identity and location.

Individual companies such as Facebook, Twitter, and other private businesses can legally control the type of content they allow. But local, state, and federal governments and agencies cannot control this content. In the United States, online hate speech has the same level of First Amendment protection as speech in other media. In the 1997 Supreme Court case *Reno v. ACLU*, the ACLU argued that two provisions of the Communications Decency Act of 1996 that criminalized sharing obscene or indecent messages was unconstitutional. The Supreme Court agreed, ruling that these two provisions were a restriction of free-speech content and therefore violated the First Amendment. With this ruling, the internet joined the list of media clearly protected by the First Amendment.

DRAWN IN:
WHY SOME CHOOSE HATE

By his own account, Christian Picciolini had lived a relatively normal childhood. He was the son of Italian immigrants who came to the United States in the mid-1960s. His parents settled into a working-class neighborhood on the South Side of Chicago. His father opened a small hair salon and later a restaurant. Like many immigrants then, they struggled to scrape by, often working fourteen hours a day, seven days a week. They took on second and third jobs to pay the bills and didn't have much time to spend with their son. Christian felt abandoned by his parents. He resented them, especially his father. As a teenager, Christian acted out to get his parents' attention. But it didn't work, and he started to withdraw from his friends and family. He didn't fit in with the other kids, and he was bullied.

One day, when Christian was fourteen, he was smoking a joint with a friend in an alley near his house. A car roared up and screeched to a stop. The car door flew open, and a man walked briskly over to them. The man was in his late twenties, with a shaved head and clenched fists. He wore tall, black combat boots

Christian Picciolini, who once led the Chicago Area Skinheads group, eventually turned away from the hate group in the mid-1990s. He started several organizations for former hate members to help them reintegrate into mainstream society.

and jeans held up by dark red suspenders. Christian thought the man looked scary and maybe a little dangerous but definitely very cool.

The stranger walked up to Christian and snatched the joint from his lips, smacking him on the back of his head. The man tossed the joint, then got right into Christian's face saying, "Don't you know that's exactly what the communists and the Jews want you to do so they can keep you docile?" Christian didn't really understand what the man was saying. He didn't really know what a Communist or a Jew was or what the word *docile* meant. He'd spent his childhood playing with his friends, trading baseball cards, and watching *Happy Days* on TV.

The stranger was Clark Martell. He was an ex-con and a violent, yet charismatic, man. After serving time in prison for attempting to firebomb the home of a Latino family, Martell founded a group called the Chicago Area Skinheads. It was one of the first neo-Nazi hate groups in the United States. Martell recruited new members by targeting marginalized teens like Christian who craved acceptance. Martell told Christian he was going to save his life.

Martell fascinated Christian. Christian wanted to be just like him. He listened to what Martell told him about the world. Martell exposed Christian to hate music, and Christian began making his own hate rock. After a while, Christian started to believe the politics of hate that Martell was preaching. He blamed Jews for what he thought was an ongoing white European genocide. He blamed blacks for the crime and violence and drugs in his city. He blamed immigrants for taking jobs from white Americans, even though his parents were also immigrants. Christian joined the Chicago Area Skinheads and became a white supremacist neo-Nazi. Christian felt empowered. He felt as if he'd become part of a new brotherhood, a cool world where he had a chance to make a difference. He even started recruiting other teen boys, luring them in with his powerful hate music. Christian also caused trouble at school. He got into fights and called his school principal, who was black, the N-word. Four schools kicked Christian out. One time, police officers led him out of school in handcuffs. He was proud of that.

In 1989 Martell was convicted of home invasion, aggravated battery, and robbery. When Martell left to serve his eleven-year prison term, sixteen-year-old Christian rose up to become head of the Chicago Area Skinheads. He was a natural leader. To form a stronger group, Christian merged it with the notoriously violent Hammerskins gang. By the time he was eighteen, Christian was recruiting new members and forming new cells all across the United States. He became even more successful when he softened the group's image and language to attract individuals who might otherwise be turned off by the harsh neo-Nazi rhetoric. Even though he softened the group's public image, Christian lived a life of hatred and violence. He described it this way:

For the next eight years [after joining the gang], I saw friends die, I saw others go to prison and inflict untold pain on countless victims and their families' lives. I heard horrific stories from young women in the movement, who'd been brutally raped by the very men they were conditioned to trust, and I myself committed acts of violence against people, solely for the color of their skin, who they loved, or the god that they prayed to. I stockpiled weapons for what I thought was an upcoming race war. I went to six high schools; I was kicked out of four of them, one of them, twice. And 25 years ago, I wrote and performed racist music that found its way to the internet decades later and partially inspired a young white nationalist [Dylann Roof] to walk into a sacred Charleston, South Carolina, church [in 2015] and senselessly massacre nine innocent people.

When he was nineteen, Picciolini met a girl from outside the white supremacist movement. They fell in love, got married, and had a son. By the time he turned twenty-two, eight years after he joined the Skinheads, Picciolini had left the life of hate behind. In 2010 he founded Life After Hate, a nonviolent, anti-racist organization. He later founded another similar organization called the Free Radicals Project. He works with fellow "formers"—former white supremacists—to help hate group members leave their movements.

WHY DO PEOPLE JOIN HATE GROUPS?

Individuals who join hate groups come from many backgrounds. Every member's journey to joining a hate group is different. And hate groups themselves differ in their goals and beliefs, so they each attract different types of people. A common stereotype of a hate group member is of a young loner, a white male with a high school education or less. However, not all members of hate groups are the same. And not all individuals who fit the profile of a typical member of a hate group are at risk of joining a hate group. The decision to join a hate group is complex.

Members of hate groups are not necessarily economically deprived. Many are solidly middle class. They come from families that are stable and from those that are not. But experts have found that children of divorce or those who are abandoned by one or more parents are more susceptible to the messages of hate groups. Peter Simi, a sociologist at Chapman University in Orange, California, notes that many hate group members have experienced child abuse, sexual abuse, or parental neglect. Still others have parents or other family members who live with substance abuse. A 2015 study from the National Consortium for the Study of Terrorism and Responses to Terrorism found that 45 percent of former white supremacist group members were victims of childhood physical abuse, with about 20 percent also being victims of childhood sexual abuse.

Some young people react to these circumstances by falling behind in school, abusing alcohol or illegal drugs, becoming violent at home or at school, or threatening suicide. Some individuals hook up with gangs or hate groups. Most people who join hate groups are young men, and they join to find meaning in their lives. They don't feel successful, they have trouble making friends, and they don't feel welcome in society. They usually feel like outcasts. Picciolini says he believes "that people become radicalized, or extremist, because they're searching for three very fundamental human needs: identity, community, and a sense of purpose." Potential members have trouble finding socially acceptable ways to fulfill these important needs from other sources.

Retired professor of psychology Ervin Staub at the University of Massachusetts–Amherst says, "Often, these are people who don't feel like they've succeeded or had a chance to succeed across normal channels of success in society. . . . If you don't feel you have much influence and power in the world, you get a sense of power from being part of a community and especially a rather militant community."

This view is echoed by many former hate group members themselves. Tony McAleer, who spent fifteen years as a recruiter and organizer for the White Aryan Resistance, relates how joining a hate

Tony McAleer was a recruiter and organizer for the neo-Nazi group White Aryan Resistance for fifteen years. In the twenty years since he left the group, McAleer has made it his mission to help former hate group members transition back into mainstream society through the organization Life After Hate.

group enhanced his sense of self-worth: "I felt power where I felt powerless. I felt a sense of belonging where I felt invisible."

Younger people tend to be especially susceptible to the appeal of hate groups. Teens who feel alienated, mistreated by their peers, bullied, or that they don't fit in are drawn to the sense of order and community that a hate group seems to provide. And experts say that teen biochemistry is still not mature. Parenting expert Dr. Deborah Gilboa says, "The teenage brain is connected strongly to emotion. These [hate] groups give them the emotional connection they are looking for." Sometimes this pull means that an individual may join a group without actually accepting the key beliefs of the hate group.

Picciolini points out that he "wasn't raised as a racist." He says that Clark Martell "gave [identity, community, and a sense of purpose] to me when I felt very powerless. And the racism actually came later."

Picciolini *learned* to hate. He and others who have joined hate groups don't necessarily start out with a shared ideology.

According to Kathleen M. Blee, a professor of sociology at the University of Pittsburgh, this is especially true for young women. "Women become associated with these groups for reasons that are cultural and social—friends, music, clothing styles—rather than because a particular racial issue is troubling them," Blee says.

Plenty of people join hate groups because they share the same prejudices and biases. These individuals genuinely hate a particular group, and they view joining a hate group as a way to justify and act on those impulses. Many people who join hate groups feel they've been victimized and view the hate group as a way to make up for that. Perhaps they've been bullied, fired from a job, or suspended from school. They blame their problems on an "other." The other is usually a member of a social group toward whom the person will eventually feel prejudice and hate. For those who join a white supremacist or other alt-right group, the "other" to blame is usually part of a minority group—black, Muslim, immigrant, or female. Simi says,

Folks who get involved in white supremacist groups feel like whites are the true victims of discrimination and that no one wants to admit it. Kids that may have been bullied, or involved in some type of interracial conflict in their lives are the ones these groups are looking for. And this is what will happen if you join their group: You'll get protection and an explanation of the conflict that you won't get from parents or school because they are part of the problem.

A. J. Marsden, an assistant professor of psychology at Beacon College in Leesburg, Florida, says that this kind of hate is based in fear—"fear of the unknown, fear of what might happen and fear of anything that's different than you or falls outside your definition of what's supposed to be normal. We establish ourselves as a tribe, and we say this is the group for which I have a love for, for which I identify with." So the hate group becomes a person's tribe, and that tribe is prejudiced against—and often not knowledgeable about—those who are not members of the tribe. As Marsden says of members of anti-Muslim groups, "There's a lot that [the members] don't know, and that scares them, because there is a small [number] of Muslims who are violent, and that is what is driving the hate."

RECRUITING NEW MEMBERS

Extremist groups have always preyed on impressionable young people. Before the internet, they reached out to new recruits through printed pamphlets, person-to-person encounters, and secret group meetings. The groups still pass out pamphlets and hold meetings, but social media offers many more ways for hate groups to recruit potential new members. As sociologist Robert Futrell of the University of Nevada–Las Vegas says, "What's different now is the range of ways the white power movement is reaching [recruits]. The internet is a boon to those who are stigmatized and relatively powerless."

Individuals are most likely to first encounter hate groups online. Hate group members are active users of Twitter, Facebook, Instagram, and other social media. They post videos on YouTube and share podcasts on their own sites and on other internet sites. Potential members may see hate group propaganda in the form of online ads or videos or shared messages from mutual friends. Some members of hate groups are even recruiting in multiplayer video games, such as Fortnite, Minecraft, and Call of Duty, by striking up online conversations with targeted users. They may start by dropping racially tinged hints about how some in-game races are superior to others. Then they may seek to push further toward racial differences in the real world.

From the propaganda on more mainstream social media and gaming sites, an individual may move on to a hate group's official website or to a general hate site, where larger groups of like-minded people are interacting. Recruiters look for these potential new members and target them by sending online messages. Some hate groups post online videos to recruit new members. These videos promote a group's cause. And they often promise that an individual will find a purpose and a sense of community if they join the group. The videos may promise a better world and a place to fit in with a group of like-minded people. Early recruitment materials are usually slick productions. They entice viewers to join the group with messaging that highlights the group's goals in a very positive light. These recruitment videos are very clever. Viewers often go on to watch more of the group's videos. Then they connect with the group online and eventually meet with a recruiter in person.

Eric "the Butcher" Fairburn performs hate music at a memorial concert for the founder of the American Nazi Party, George Lincoln Rockwell, on August 27, 2005. Fairburn was a racist skinhead and a member of one of the most infamous hate music bands in the United States. He is now serving life in prison for the murder of a homeless black man in Indianapolis, Indiana.

Each organization has its own tools for attracting new members. For example, some hate groups promote their messages through hate music based on familiar punk or metal sounds but with more violent lyrics. Hate music is big business, worth millions of dollars a year in CD sales and royalties. Extremists can find hate music on the internet, and live concerts are a meeting ground for recruiters to connect with potential members.

However a person first encounters a hate group, it all leads up to making personal contact. The initial in-person contacts aren't usually one-on-one meetings. Several people from the group meet a potential member to figure out what the recruit might bring to the organization. The members want to know if a person is physically tough, offers website-building skills, or knows other people who might also be good recruits. They also want to make sure that the new person is not actually a law enforcement plant, someone who is trying to get into the group to help the police or the FBI break it up or undermine their plans. And the hate group members want the person to feel that their group is a group worth joining. Hate groups know that welcoming and bonding with new members will make them want to spend more time with the group. That is why in-person meetings are still an important part of recruitment.

Once a group's main recruiter and other group members approve a new person, that recruit is invited to group meetings and functions. The new person will start to receive group emails, tweets, and information about online forums. Hate groups proceed slowly with new recruits, to build a deepening sense of commitment and loyalty to the group and its larger mission. Eventually, the new person might be asked to recruit their friends to the group. A person gets sucked in, little by little, until the group becomes an inescapable part of that person's life. From the first online contact to the eventual admittance into the group, it's a well-planned, well-executed seduction. The new member might never see it coming.

RESISTING RECRUITMENT

Human beings are social creatures by nature. Feeling the need for a sense of connection to a larger group is a normal human need. It does not mean a person will automatically join an extremist hate group. But if a person is lonely and looking for a sense of purpose, that person can be vulnerable to hate group tactics. Being aware of their methods and keeping a sharp eye out for the true intentions of online connections are key to resisting hate group recruitment. Always look deeper into the true philosophies and messages of any organization before joining. Most hate groups won't hit a potential recruit with the hard-core ideology right away. They will offer a softer message that might sound reasonable at first. Thinking critically and staying aware are very important in understanding the message. For example, hate groups try to convince potential new members that joining the group will improve their life or help them deal with anger. Finding healthy ways of dealing with problems and insecurities makes any individual stronger and more able to resist the pull of hate groups.

If an individual is being recruited locally, it's a good idea for that person to report what's happening to someone they trust. If the recruiter is a fellow student—or, just as likely, a former student—report the interaction to a teacher or school counselor. The reporting can be done anonymously, if necessary. Telling adults or authorities that a dangerous activity is taking place is an important way of stopping the spread of hate groups. Even if the hate group is not successful in recruiting one person, it will try to recruit someone else.

The most effective way to actively avoid recruitment is to recognize the potential for personal biases and combat them through knowledge. Hate groups target victims who are different from themselves. They usually target minorities. Many members of a hate group have never formed a personal relationship with or even talked to a person from a group they hate. Seeking conversations with people from different backgrounds helps build understanding and can create relationships that prevent or overturn bias.

In November 2015, members of the Islamic State of Iraq and Syria (known as ISIS) launched a series of terrorist attacks in Paris, France. That December self-radicalized Islamic extremists in San Bernardino, California, began shooting in a holiday office party at a social services center, killing fourteen and wounding twenty-two. With these attacks, Islamophobia gained strength in the United States. Muslim Americans Sebastian Robins and Mona Haydar knew the danger to their family

Muslim Americans Sebastian Robins and Mona Haydar are proud to join in the fight against hate and bias in the United States. Founders of "Ask a Muslim," the couple participated in a 2017 fund-raiser in New York City for Syrian refugees.

and Muslim friends. They wanted to act. "We felt like we had to do something to replace some of that trauma with love and connection," Haydar recalled. The couple set up a makeshift "Ask a Muslim" booth outside their local public library in Cambridge, Massachusetts. They offered free coffee, doughnuts, and flowers for those willing to stop and talk. Passersby stopped and asked Haydar and Robins about everything from potty training their son to what it is like to be a Muslim American in modern times. Overall, Haydar said, "It was a lot of curiosity and a lot of joy." "Ask a Muslim" went viral, exposing more Americans to people they might not otherwise have come to know. Education is a powerful tool to combat hate.

CHAPTER 7

RESIST:
COMBATING HATE

Billings is the largest town in the sparsely populated state of Montana. Like any other town, it has strip malls, gas stations, schools, and churches. And like a lot of other towns across the United States, Billings is a fairly homogeneous (uniform) community, where most people are of the same race. As of the most recent 2010 census, just over 90 percent of the population of Billings, Montana, is white. This percentage is just about the same as it was at the end of the twentieth century. According to census data from 1990, Billings had about eighty-one thousand residents. Of those people, only about twenty-five hundred were Latinos. About four hundred residents were black people, and about one hundred were Jews. As in any community, not everyone got along, but people treated one another with respect. It was a relatively peaceful town.

In 1986 white supremacist Richard Butler convinced a group of white supremacists called the Aryan Congress to create a "homeland" to unite white people and white hate groups across the United States. The plan was to take over five northwestern states: Idaho, Oregon, Washington, Wyoming, and Montana. Butler chose these states because they have few minorities. He also thought law enforcement was weak in those states and that white citizens there would support his racist ideology.

Over the next few years, members of various white supremacist groups began to move to the wide-open spaces of Montana. Slowly but steadily, members of the Ku Klux Klan, the White Aryan Resistance, the Christian Patriots, and other white power groups began to move to Billings and other surrounding towns. Hate literature started to appear in Billings in 1992. The following year, people attending a Martin Luther King Jr. Day celebration found KKK flyers under the windshield wipers of their cars. And the hate only increased. Later that year, the words "Nuke Israel" were spray-painted on a stop sign. Headstones at a local Jewish cemetery were pushed over. White supremacists interrupted a Sunday service at the African Methodist Episcopal Wyman Chapel to intimidate its black congregation. And the home of an interracial couple (white and American Indian) was vandalized.

It all came to a head on December 2, 1993. That day someone threw a piece of cinder block through a window at the home of Brian and Tammie Schnitzer, one of the town's Jewish families. The window was in the bedroom of the couple's five-year-old son Isaac, who was not there at the time. Tammie Schnitzer reported the crime to the police. To her dismay, the officer in charge advised her to take down the family's Hanukkah decorations to avoid drawing further attention to their Jewish identity. (Hanukkah is an eight-day Jewish holiday that celebrates the rededication of the Holy Temple in Jerusalem.) She told this story to a reporter from the local *Billings Gazette* newspaper. She told the reporter how troubled she was by the officer's advice. "Maybe it's not wise to keep these symbols up," she said. "But how do you explain that to a child?"

Reading about the incident in the newspaper, residents of Billings were equally troubled, and they took action. Margaret MacDonald, a forty-two-year-old mother with two small children, worked with the minister of her church, the First Congregational Church of the United Church of Christ. They found menorahs (candelabras for Hanukkah celebrations) that members of their congregation could put in their windows to show solidarity with the Schnitzers. The *Billings Gazette* also printed a full-page picture of a menorah that readers could cut out and use. The town joined in the movement and put menorahs in their windows. Billings, as a community, united against hate.

The displays of Jewish symbols by Christian households enraged the hate groups, and they lashed out. They broke glass panes in the door of a local Methodist church that displayed the menorah pictures. They fired shots at a local Catholic school that was supporting the anti-hate campaign. They kicked out the windows of six cars parked in front of houses displaying menorahs.

The townspeople of Billings, Montana, placed menorahs in their windows to show solidarity with the victims of a targeted attack against a Jewish family during the Hanukkah season in 1993. The residents' message was clear: not in our town.

The homeowners received anonymous phone calls saying, "Go look at your car, Jew-lover." With every act of violence and intimidation, the anti-hate movement grew. What started with a few dozen supportive citizens expanded into a display of more than six thousand pictures of menorahs.

MacDonald later reflected on the response: "All along, our coalition had been saying an attack on one of us is an attack on all of us. And God bless them, the people of this town understood." The residents of Billings stood up to every act of vandalism and violence. It took several months, but eventually the Klan and the skinheads and all the other white supremacists grew quiet. The vandalism stopped, the hate-filled flyers disappeared, and the anonymous phone calls ended.

LEAVING A HATE GROUP

Many hate group members choose to leave their groups and, in some cases, abandon hatred and prejudice. Leaving a hate group is a difficult decision. Often some major event triggers it, such as having a fight with the group leader or watching a close friend in the organization get arrested or hurt. Some people who leave hate groups do so because they change and no longer hold the same biases and prejudices. Others who leave hate groups hold on to their prejudices but tire of the violence and danger that is a part of being an active member of a hate group. Still other hate group members grow away from the organization as their lives change. For example, many ex-members have said that getting married and having children changed their perspective. They don't have the same amount of time to devote to the group or don't want to risk the safety of their loved ones.

However, outsiders can rarely force a member to leave. Tony McAleer, former white supremacist and cofounder of Life After Hate, says that for devoted hate group members "ideology and identity have become the same. When you challenge ideology, you're challenging [a person's sense of self]. It's not so much changing their minds, it's [changing] their hearts." Usually the decision to leave a hate group comes from the member. And it is a tough journey, even if an individual is committed to it.

Former Ku Klux Klansman Shane Johnson followed in his family's tradition by joining the Klan. Leaving the group was difficult. To move forward, Johnson focused on his new family and the support of Life After Hate.

Most groups don't make it easy for members to leave. Departing members are likely to face resistance from group leaders and other members. That resistance may be significant—and may even put the person at risk of physical harm. Shane Johnson joined a rural chapter of the Ku Klux Klan in northern Indiana when he was fourteen. Joining the Klan was a family tradition. Johnson's father and many of his father's relatives were KKK members. "We were known as a Klan family," he said years later.

Johnson was an active Klan member for about six years. He had a drinking problem, and when he was in his early twenties, he was arrested for a drunken fight in a nearby town. Following the arrest, he stopped drinking and decided to drop out of the Klan. Speaking of the reaction of other Klan members and his own family, he says, "When I dropped out, they beat the holy hell out of me."

Johnson found support from the group Life After Hate. Founded and run by Christian Picciolini and other former hate group members, the organization is one of many that helps people like Johnson leave hate groups. The Free Radicals Project, also founded and led by Christian Picciolini, is a similar group. It works with individuals and their families to pull away safely from hate groups and their extremist ideologies. In Johnson's case, he also found help and support from a woman named Tiffany Gregoire, who helped him question the reasons for his hate-filled belief system and reevaluate the world. He realized that he needed to take personal responsibility for his own problems. Although he still receives threats from Klansmen, Johnson and Gregoire are now focused on their family and raising their son.

Belonging to a hate group is an intense, all-consuming experience. Leaving a hate group can be just as intense. As former neo-Nazi Angela King tells it, the change encompasses every aspect of your life from the mental to the physical. "People in extremist groups wrap their entire identities around it. Everything in their life has to be changed, from the way they think, to the people they associate with, to dealing with permanent tattoos," King says. An individual leaving a group has to change his or her whole life. Some people compare it to belonging to a cult or to living with an addiction. In the same way that support groups are important to people who want to leave a cult or kick an addiction, they are also vital for helping people leave hate groups. Anti-hate group organizations, church groups, community service groups, and groups of supportive family and friends run support groups for former hate group members. The support groups help former members make changes to their lifestyles.

Changes in any behavior are difficult to make. For people in hate groups, it is especially challenging to overcome prejudice. Experts know, for example, that a person doesn't just stop hating from one day to the next. And because hatred lingers, the person trying to leave the hate group is at risk for some time of returning to it. Peter Simi has interviewed many former hate group members. He has found that "a lot of them talk about being addicted to hate." Persistence is key to staying out of hate organizations once a member has left.

Picciolini says that support, understanding, and compassion are powerful tools to offer someone who wants to leave a hate group. He says that "all of us who left [a hate group] received compassion from the people we least deserved it from when we least deserved it. It's the [acceptance] of the people we hated when we don't deserve it that helps people get out."

Connecting with someone from a once-hated group is an important part of healing. Sociologist Michael Kimmel notes that many former hate group members had "met a member of the despised group, one . . . individual whose very existence eroded all their categorical group stereotypes, [and] they began to unlearn the dehumanization the movement had taught them."

Frank Meeink, a former neo-Nazi who went to prison for kidnapping a rival skinhead, began to move away from his hate group because he wanted to have a chance to see his young daughter—something he knew he couldn't do if he returned to prison. However, he did not begin to change his opinions until Keith Brookstein, who is Jewish, hired the swastika-tattooed neo-Nazi to move antique furniture around his business. Brookstein told Meeink that he didn't care if he was a neo-Nazi, as long as he didn't damage the furniture. Meeink spent many hours working and talking with Brookstein. His views about Jews slowly evolved. A big moment came when Meeink broke a piece of furniture. He told Brookstein about it, thinking he'd be fired. Instead, Brookstein told Meeink that he was a smart asset to the company and that he still had a job. "I was walking home that day," Meeink said, "and I was just like, 'You know what? I can't keep claiming I'm a neo-Nazi. I couldn't kill Keith. I would f**king probably take a bullet for Keith now,' and so I started to change."

Hate members leaving their group must also deal with the potential for physical harm from the group itself. Established anti-hate organizations can help with advice for the best approaches to cutting

STUDENTS RESPOND TO HATE

Incidents of hate-inspired vandalism surged, including in schools, following the election of Trump as president of the United States. On November 16, 2016, students at Attleboro High School (AHS) in Attleboro, Massachusetts, found racist graffiti scrawled in the third-floor boys' restroom. The graffiti said "Go Donald Trump," as well as "KKK will handle all n****rs."

The school removed the offending comments, and one month later, students responded by countering the hate with kindness. More than sixty volunteers handwrote "love notes" to each of the high school's seventeen hundred students and staff members. The notes, written on index cards, expressed the students' heartfelt appreciation and respect for their fellow students. The cards were on their desks when they arrived at school first thing in the morning.

"The message is to bring the community together and show we are supportive and care about everyone," said senior Iffa Sugrio.

Fellow student Dylan Ilkowitz agreed, saying, "Our goal is to make every student feel that AHS is an inclusive environment and that our school did not stand for racist and prejudiced values."

No further incidents of graffiti have been reported.

all ties with an organization. This might involve changing a phone number and getting a new mailing address to prevent the group from contacting them. Depending on the financial circumstances of the individual leaving the group and the level of physical danger they may face, an anti-hate organization might recommend moving to a new home. Cutting off all means of contact from the old hate group will help a member move forward safely and effectively. It may also be a good idea to hire a lawyer familiar with hate-related issues. A lawyer can make sure that all legal ties to the organization are cut off.

STANDING UP TO HATE GROUPS

If a hate group enters or becomes active in your community, what can you do about it? The solution isn't always simple or easy, but it always starts with one thing: resistance.

Resistance was the backbone of the anti-hate group movement in Billings, Montana. In 2018 Sarah Anthony, former chair of the Billings Coalition for Human Rights, reflected on what Billings had done in the mid-1990s to combat hate:

> Come up with a plan. Make a few phone calls. Put up menorahs. That's all we did. Pretty simple stuff, actually. But you have to build the sentiment, to forge the real feeling that goes deep. We did something right here, and we will do it again if we have to. If we don't, there are people who would break every window in Billings, and we would look out those windows and see ourselves.

Experts point out that when hate rears its head, a community cannot ignore it and hope it will go away. Apathy and avoidance allow hate to take root and grow. It has to be confronted head-on.

The Anti-Defamation League and Southern Poverty Law Center are excellent resources that provide a starting point for what you can do to combat hate. The Southern Poverty Law Center offers a community response guide that outlines ten ways to fight hate groups. The steps are

1. Act.
2. Join forces.
3. Support the victims.
4. Speak up.
5. Educate yourself.
6. Create an alternative.
7. Pressure leaders.
8. Stay engaged.
9. Teach acceptance.
10. Dig deeper.

Following these guidelines, the first thing to do is to report any experience of hate speech or hate crime. Pick up the phone, and call your local authorities. If you don't feel safe doing that, tell a trusted adult, such as a neighbor or family member, counselor, or a leader in your church, synagogue, or mosque. If the hate is happening at your school, tell your school principal, counselor, or school resource officer. Post about it on social media. Contact your friends and family. Organize a neighborhood or community meeting. Reach out to the Anti-Defamation League or the Southern Poverty Law Center. Do something to combat the hate you see.

Next, get involved in fixing the damage the hate group caused. Volunteer to repair acts of vandalism. Paint over offensive graffiti. Make sure victims are taken care of. Often hate crimes don't target specific individuals. They target an entire group or community. So if hate members vandalize a mosque or a synagogue, everyone in the community suffers. In Madison, Wisconsin, in 2017, for example, a small local synagogue was the victim of a hate crime. Less than twenty-four hours before the start of the Jewish holiday of Rosh Hashanah, red swastikas and the words "Trump Rules" and "Antifa Sucks" were found

City worker Cal Steinberg removed spray-painted hate symbols on a marker outside a historic synagogue in Madison, Wisconsin, shortly after they were discovered in the fall of 2017.

CONFRONTING HATE AND STAYING SAFE

Hate groups are persistent and often violent. Resistance typically increases the levels of threats and violence. The groups often target leaders of the resistance for specific verbal and physical attacks. This is especially true when the resistance is led by members of a minority group targeted by the hate group. So hate groups or members of those groups should not be confronted directly. Confrontation can escalate quickly into violence, and violence won't change minds. Former neo-Nazi Frank Meeink recalls his reaction when he was showered with rocks and bottles while marching in a KKK parade: "I never once ducked a bottle and thought 'Woah, I better rethink my belief system here.' Instead, it was, 'Now I'm angry. Now I have an enemy I can see.'"

It is better to react in peace to the actual or implied violence of hate groups. Take the high ground and stand it. You don't have to prove how strong you are by engaging in violence of your own. Showing strength through peace is not only safer but also more effective.

spray-painted on a memorial next to the synagogue. Park officials removed the offensive content before the beginning of Rosh Hashanah services began, and the rest of the community sprang into action. In response, the community placed flowers at the site, and students at the University of Wisconsin–Madison campus, along with city leaders, denounced the vandalism.

Like the Madison residents, do whatever you can to make a stand against hate. Remember, you aren't alone. In fact, facing a hate group alone may be dangerous, so work with friends and neighbors to stand up to a hate group. Work together to repair your community and support the victims of hate. Organize a rally at your school or participate in one in your community. Large groups and the power of people can be very effective in driving out hate.

Other ideas include making and distributing flyers and posters that promote a message of tolerance and peace. Work with friends, local religious congregations, community groups, and other organizations. Write letters to the online editors of local papers, contact your local TV and radio stations, and spread your message on social media. The stronger and the more consistent the public pressure for a hate group to stop its actions, the more likely it is the group will stop.

TAKING LEGAL ACTION

First Amendment rights legally protect many kinds of hate group activity. But some things that hate groups do are illegal. For example, damaging or defacing property is against the law, whether it's breaking a window, painting offensive graffiti on a wall, or burning down a garage. Physical attacks are also against the law. If one or more members of a hate group physically attack someone, the attack is illegal. Vandalism, graffiti, and physical attacks should all be reported to authorities by calling 9-1-1. Even small things should be reported. Reporting a hate group for something small may stop something more violent from happening in the future.

Sometimes, if the hate does not stop and the crimes are especially offensive, community leaders and other individuals may choose to report local hate groups to a national organization, such as the Southern Poverty Law Center or the Anti-Defamation League. These organizations use their legal teams to go after hate groups to break them up.

Heidi Beirich, leader of the Southern Poverty Law Center's Intelligence Project, has filed lawsuits against multiple branches of hate groups. In 2016 she commented about the project's success at breaking up KKK groups through financial methods. "We came up with this idea that we should sue these folks in civil court [a court that handles legal disputes that are not crimes] to bankrupt them," she says. When a group loses a civil suit, the penalty is usually a very high fine. If it is high enough, it can put a business or organization out of business. The Intelligence Project has successfully stopped a series of Klan groups that

"IT'S HARD TO HATE SOMEBODY YOU KNOW"

In 2013 fourteen-year-old Ziad Ahmed, a Bangladeshi American Muslim from Princeton, New Jersey, created a website called redefy (www.redefy.org). The site provides a space for people to share their experiences dealing with hate and prejudices. He wants his peers to know that it's not acceptable to put other people down because of their race, views, or religion.

Ziad was inspired by his experience as a Muslim in post-9/11 America. "From a young age, I knew I was different because of my faith," he said. "I remember one time in sixth grade, someone asked me if Islam meant that I worshipped a monkey god, as a joke, and I remember being so upset." By encouraging visitors to his site to share their personal stories, Ziad hopes to educate others and spread tolerance. As he says, "It's hard to hate somebody you know . . . just because people have different sexual orientation, different skin color, different gender, it doesn't make someone less or different."

they have sued. One suit resulted in a $2.5 million judgment against the Imperial Klans of America, the second-largest KKK group in the United States, based in Dawson Springs, Kentucky. Although the Imperial Klans of America is still operational, the organization is now much smaller. Beirich goes on to explain, "When these groups don't have money, that means there's less violence that they could perpetrate. The whole idea is to not allow them to function."

LOVE VS. HATE: TEACHING TOLERANCE

Defeating one hate group does not defeat them all. Experts with the Southern Poverty Law Center and the Anti-Defamation League say that it is a constant struggle to fight the growing number of hate groups in the United States. To effectively combat hate groups, hate speech, and hate crimes, society must ultimately deal with the underlying issues that lead to the spread of hate.

Sociologists and other experts have studied prejudice, and they know that it is learned early in life. For children who hear racist, homophobic, misogynist (anti-woman), anti-Semitic, Islamophobic, or otherwise intolerant language—on television, on the internet, and from friends and family—chances are higher that the child will grow up with the same prejudices. Researchers have found that by the age of three or four, children of one race show preference for other children of the same race. Gender stereotypes are established in children by the time they turn ten. For the cycle of prejudice to end, children must learn tolerance and acceptance—in daycares, in schools, in community organizations, and through the media.

Many schools are adopting antibias education curricula. Antibias education involves exposing students to people of different races, nationalities, and religions. It encourages young people to look at others and admire their uniqueness and their sameness. It's all about learning how not to be prejudiced against others. One of the best ways

In August 2018, white supremacists across the United States gathered to mark the anniversary of the Unite the Right rally in Charlottesville, Virginia. In Washington, DC, their numbers were dwarfed by hundreds of thousands of counterprotesters (*above*) united against hate and prejudice.

to learn to be accepting of others is to get to know them. Many whites who are prejudiced against blacks have never gotten to know a black person. Similarly, many people who hate LGBTQI peoples have never knowingly hung out with someone who is gay or transgender. Research shows that when a person meets and gets to know something about someone who is different from them, they gain a better understanding of the other person. They begin to rethink existing prejudices. The more we meet, work, study, play, and socialize with people who do not share our same experiences and backgrounds, the more likely we are to accept differences and build on similarities.

The bottom line is that hate lessens when we learn about and practice tolerance with our fellow human beings. Prejudice leads to hate. Love leads to the tolerance and acceptance that makes any society strong and enduring. The best and most effective way to defeat hate is by practicing and performing acts of love and compassion.

GLOSSARY

alt-left: short for "alternative left," an umbrella label for politically left-wing extremist groups

alt-right: short for "alternative right," an umbrella label for various politically right-wing extremist groups

antifa: short for "anti-fascist," a label for left-wing hate groups that oppose fascist and other right-wing groups

anti-immigrant: hostile to or prejudiced against immigrants, especially from nonwhite, non-European countries

anti-Muslim: hostile to or prejudiced against Muslims, both within and outside a country's borders. Muslims are followers of Islam, a religion founded in the seventh century CE by the prophet Muhammad.

anti-Semitic: hostile to or prejudiced against Jews

Aryan: people of northern European and western Asian heritage. White supremacists view the Aryan race as superior to all others.

bias incident: an offensive action, speech, or expression motivated by bias against a race, ethnicity, religion, or gender that does not break the law

black separatism: a left-wing movement that seeks separate economic and cultural development for people of African descent

Christian dominionism: also known as dominion theology, a right-wing political and religious movement that seeks to form a nation governed by Christians and Christian theology

Christian Identity: a racist and white supremacist interpretation of Christianity that believes only whites of northern European descent are the chosen people

civil rights movement: a social movement of the 1950s and 1960s that fought to gain equal rights for black Americans

conservatism: also known as right wing, this political ideology holds to traditional values and attitudes about family, gender, and sexual orientation. Conservatives also believe in small government.

ethnostate: a nation made up of and governed by a specific ethnic group

fascism: a political ideology or movement that puts loyalty to nation and race above loyalty to the individual. Fascism is a form of government with a dictator as the supreme ruler.

First Amendment: the first article of the Bill of Rights (the first ten amendments to the US Constitution), which guarantees freedom of speech and freedom of religion

hate crime: a criminal offense motivated by the offender's bias against an entire race, religion, disability, sexual orientation, ethnicity, gender, or gender identity

hate group: an organization that is prejudiced against and takes actions against an entire race, religion, disability, sexual orientation, ethnicity, gender, or gender identity

hate speech: offensive speech or actions that result from a prejudice against an entire race, religion, disability, sexual orientation, ethnicity, gender, or gender identity

Holocaust denial: the belief that the Holocaust of World War II, in which Nazi Germany systematically murdered six million Jews and other "undesirables," never occurred or was not as large as historians and survivors claim

homophobia: hostility, fear, or prejudice against people attracted to the same sex

Islamophobia: hostility, fear, or prejudice against Muslims (people who follow Islam)

Ku Klux Klan (KKK): an American white supremacist hate group founded after the Civil War to intimidate black Americans and prevent them from exercising their legal rights. The KKK remains a notable white supremacist group in the United States in the twenty-first century.

LGBTQI: an acronym that refers to lesbian, gay, bisexual, transgender, queer or questioning, and intersex individuals

liberalism: also known as left wing, this political ideology allows for flexible definitions of family, gender, sexual orientation, and religious faith. Liberals generally believe in the ability of government to do good, and they support government intervention as a way to help people in need and to ensure equality throughout society.

militia: a body of citizens that organizes for unofficial military service

millennialism: the Christian religious belief that the world is about to enter into the time of Tribulation, a battle between good and evil after which Jesus will return to Earth

nationalism: a political ideology and movement, typically right wing, that believes that one's own country is inherently superior to all others

National Socialism: another name for Nazism. The Nazi Party in early twentieth-century Germany was officially known as the National Socialist Party.

Nazism: originating in twentieth-century Germany, this right-wing political ideology and movement combines fascism, nationalism, racism, and anti-Semitism. In twentieth-century Germany, Adolf Hitler led that nation as its Nazi dictator from 1933 until his death in 1945.

neo-Confederate: a political movement that supports the ideology of the former Confederate States of America, which existed in the southern part of the United States from 1861 until the end of the Civil War in 1865. The Confederacy upheld the belief in white superiority and allowed for slavery as a legal institution.

neo-Nazi: a right-wing political movement that supports the racist and anti-Semitic ideology of Nazi Germany

propaganda: ideas, facts, or allegations spread deliberately to further a particular cause or to damage an opposing cause

racism: prejudice, discrimination, or hatred directed at another race, based on the belief that one's own race is superior to all others

racist skinhead movement: a violent offshoot of the white supremacist movement. Members are identified by their short hair and militaristic clothing.

white nationalism: a right-wing political ideology and movement that promotes the concept of an all-white or majority-white nation. It also aims to suppress what the movement believes are inferior nonwhite minorities.

white supremacism: a right-wing political ideology and movement that believes that whites are superior to all other races and ethnicities

xenophobia: hostility, fear, or prejudice against people from other countries

SOURCE NOTES

7   "Frequently Asked Questions about Hate Groups," Southern Poverty Law Center, October 4, 2017, https://www.splcenter.org/20171004/frequently -asked-questions-about-hate-groups#hate group.

9   Lynn Hulsey, "Groups like the KKK Preach White Power but Shun 'Hate' Label," *Dayton (OH) Daily News*, August 18, 2017, https://www .mydaytondailynews.com/news/crime--law/groups-like-the-kkk-preach -white-power-but-shun-hate-label/U9JCYBPpBFHimNHlPObpdP/.

12 James B. Taylor, *Virginia Baptist Ministers* (Philadelphia: Lippincott, 1859), 164.

13 Jarvis Keiley, "Georgia," *The Catholic Encyclopedia*, vol. 6 (New York: Robert Appleton, 1909), accessed April 4, 2018, http://www.newadvent.org /cathen/06460a.htm.

13 Jarvis Keiley, "South Carolina," *The Catholic Encyclopedia*, vol. 14 (New York: Robert Appleton, 1912), accessed April 4, 2018, http://www .newadvent.org/cathen/14157a.htm.

14 U.S. Const. amend. I

16 John F. Kennedy, "Transcript: JFK's Speech on His Religion," September 13, 1960, *NPR*, December 5, 2007, https://www.npr.org/templates/story /story.php?storyId=16920600.

18 Kwame Ture and Charles V. Hamilton, *Black Power: The Politics of Liberation in America* (New York: Random House), 1967, 4.

23 "About," Black Lives Matter, accessed August 27, 2018, https://www .blacklivesmatter.com/about/.

28 "Alert over Gay Plague," *Daily Telegraph* (London), May 2, 1983.

29 Gregory M. Herek, quoted in Haeyoun Park and Iaryna Mykhyalyshyn, "L.G.B.T. People Are More Likely to Be Targets of Hate Crimes Than Any Other Minority Group," *New York Times*, June 16, 2016, https://www .nytimes.com/interactive/2016/06/16/us/hate-crimes-against-lgbt.html.

33 Jussi Halla-aho, quoted in David Dunne, "Finns Party MP Remains Defiant after Race Hate Conviction," *Helsinki Times*, June 20, 2012, http:// www.helsinkitimes.fi/helsinkitimes/2012jun/issue24-255/helsinki _times24-255.pdf .

34–35 Soldiers of Odin USA, Facebook, accessed June 7, 2018, https://www .facebook.com/soldiersofodinusaofficial.

35 Jack Maskell. "Qualifications for President and the 'Natural Born' Citizenship Eligibility Requirement," CRS Report for Congress, November 14, 2011, https://fas.org/sgp/crs/misc/R42097.pdf.

35 Omarosa Manigault Newman, quoted in Michael D. Shear and Eileen Sullivan, "Trump Calls Omarosa Manigault Newman 'That Dog' in His Latest Insult," *New York Times*, August 14, 2018, https://www.nytimes.com/2018/08/14/us/politics/trump-omarosa-dog.html.

36 Alexia Underwood, "What Most Americans Get Wrong about Islamophobia," Vox, April 6, 2018, https://www.vox.com/2018/4/6/17169448/trump-islamophobia-muslims-islam-black-lives-matter.

36 Claire Galofaro, Associated Press, "Trump Rise Put Spark to Long-Simmering Racism, Experts Say," *Portland (ME) Press Herald*, August 13, 2017, https://www.pressherald.com/2017/08/13/trump-rise-put-spark-to-long-simmering-racism-experts-say-white-supremacy-has-always-lurked-in-the-shadows-of-america-but-now-its-actively-trying-to-move-into-the-mainstream/.

37 Rokia Hassanein, "'Making America Hate Again'—the Correlation between Trump's Anti-Muslim Tweets and Hate Crimes," Americans United, July 24, 2018, https://www.au.org/blogs/wall-of-separation/making-america-hate-again-the-correlation-between-trumps-anti-muslim.

37 German Lopez, "The Sneaky Language Today's Politicians Use to Get Away with Racism and Sexism," Vox, February 1, 2016, https://www.vox.com/2016/2/1/10889138/coded-language-thug-bossy.

37 Esther J. Cepeda, "We Can All Hear Trump's Dog Whistles to Racists," Al Día News, May 30, 2018, http://www.aldianews.com/articles/opinion/we-can-all-hear-trumps-dog-whistles-racists/52801.

37 Lopez, "Sneaky Language."

39 "Our Mission," Anti-Defamation League, accessed March 6, 2018, https://www.adl.org/who-we-are/our-mission.

42 Emily Nicolosi, quoted in Ashley Imlay, "Geography of Hate: U. Study Examines Hate Groups Based on Religion," *Salt Lake City Deseret News*, February 11, 2018, https://www.deseretnews.com/article/900010002/geography-of-hate-u-study-examines-hate-groups-based-on-region.html.

43 Nicolosi, quoted in Lisa Potter, "Drivers of Hate in the U.S. Have Distinct Regional Differences," University of Utah, February 9, 2018, https://unews.utah.edu/drivers-of-hate-in-the-u-s-have-distinct-regional-differences/.

44 Jonathan A. Greenblatt, quoted in "ADL Report: White Supremacist Murders More Than Doubled in 2017," Anti-Defamation League, January 17, 2018, https://www.adl.org/news/press-releases/adl-report-white-supremacist-murders-more-than-doubled-in-2017.

47 "ISD Quotes: Quotes by and from Ian Stuart Donaldson," Blood and Honour Worldwide, accessed February 27, 2018, http://www.bloodandhonourworldwide.co.uk/bhww/isd/isd-quotes/.

52 Brigitte Gabriel, quoted at Joint Forces Staff College lecture, June 2007, broadcast on C-SPAN, ACT for America, accessed August 29, 2018, https://www.actforamerica.org.

58 "Report: New Black Panther Party for Self Defense (NBPP)," Anti-Defamation League, accessed June 8, 2018, https://www.adl.org /resources/reports/report-new-black-panther-party-for-self-defense-nbpp ?referrer=https%3A//www.google.co.uk/#.V4H-bLerTcs.

60 Asher Schnecter, "What Are the '14 Words' Everyone's Been Freaking Out About?," *Haaretz*, January 6, 2017, https://www.haaretz.com/us-news/what -are-the-14-words-everyones-been-freaking-out-about-1.5482606.

65 Oren Segal, quoted in Joe Sterling and Nicole Chavez, "What's the 'Alt-Left?' Experts Say It's a 'Made-Up Term,'" *CNN*, August 16, 2017, https://www.cnn.com/2017/08/16/politics/what-is-alt-left/index.htm.

66 Scott Bronstein and Drew Griffin, "Video Shows White Teens Driving over, Killing Black Man, Says DA," *CNN*, August 8, 2011, http://www.cnn .com/2011/CRIME/08/06/mississippi.hate.crime/index.html.

68 Bronstein and Griffin.

68 Bronstein and Griffin.

69 "Hate Crimes," Federal Bureau of Investigation, February 8, 2017, https:// www.fbi.gov/investigate/civil-rights/hate-crimes.

69–70 Hate Crimes Statistics Act, 28 USC § 534.

75–76 Civil Rights Act of 1968, Pub.L. 90–284, 82 Stat. 73.

76 California Penal Code § 190.2.

78 Gadeir Abbas, quoted in "U.S. Anti-Muslim Hate Crimes Rose 15 Percent in 2017: Advocacy Group," Reuters, April 23, 2018, https://www.reuters .com/article/us-usa-islam-hatecrime/u-s-anti-muslim-hate-crimes-rose-15 -percent-in-2017-advocacy-group-idUSKBN1HU240.

78 Maxine Bernstein, "Man Accused in MAX Attack Confessed to Stabbing, Said 'I'm Happy Now. I'm Happy Now,'" *Portland Oregonian*, May 30, 2017, https://www.oregonlive.com/portland/index.ssf/2017/05/man _accused_in_max_attack_cont.html.

78 Bernstein.

78 Donald Trump, Twitter post, May 29, 2017, 7:51 a.m., https://twitter.com /potus/status/869204433418280961?lang=en.

80 "Terrorism," Federal Bureau of Investigation, accessed March 26, 2018, https://www.fbi.gov/investigate/terrorism.

82 *The Holy Bible, English Standard Version*, text edition, 2016, https://www .biblegateway.com/passage/?search=Leviticus+18%3A22&version=ESV.

82–83 Fred Phelps, *9/11: God's Wrath Revealed* video, September 8, 2006, http://www.godhatesfags.com/video/videonews.html.

84 Albert Snyder, quoted in Sean Gregory, "Why the Supreme Court Ruled for Westboro," *Time*, March 3, 2011, http://content.time.com/time/nation/article/0,8599,2056613,00.html.

85 John Roberts, quoted in 562 U.S. 443 (2011).

85 *Merriam-Webster's*, "hate speech," accessed August 30, 2018, https://www.merriam-webster.com/dictionary/hate%20speech.

86 "Declaration of Independence: A Transcription," National Archives, accessed January 15, 2018, https://www.archives.gov/founding-docs/declaration-transcript.

86 Benjamin Franklin (as Silence Dogood), "Silence Dogood, No. 8," *New England Current*, July 9, 1722, https://founders.archives.gov/documents/Franklin/01-01-02-0015.

86 George Washington, "Address to the Officers of the Army," George Washington's Mount Vernon, March 15, 1783, https://www.mountvernon.org/george-washington/quotes/article/for-if-men-are-to-be-precluded-from-offering-their-sentiments-on-a-matter-which-may-involve-the-most-serious-and-alarming-consequences-that-can-invite-the-consideration-of-mankind-reason-is-of-no-use-to-us-the-freedom-of-speech-may-be-taken-away-and-dumb-/.

86 Brandenburg v. Ohio, 395 U.S. 444 (1969).

87 Ohio Rev.Code Ann. § 2923.13.

87 Ohio Rev.Code Ann.

87–88 Walter Isaacson, "The Two Original Sins of the Internet—and Why We Must Fix Them," *Aspen Journal of Ideas*, March/April 2016, http://www.aspen.us/journal/editions/marchapril-2016/two-original-sins-internet-%E2%80%94-and-why-we-must-fix-them.

90 Danish Penal Code § 266b.

93 Michael Barfield, quoted in Jacob Ogles, "Identifying a Lawful Rally from a Violent Angry Hate Mob," *Advocate*, August 22, 2017, https://www.advocate.com/race/2017/8/22/identifying-lawful-rally-violent-angry-hate-mob.

94 Gab, accessed March 30, 2018, https://www.gab.ai Gab.

94 "Community Standards: Objectionable Content," Facebook, accessed September 7, 2018, https://www.facebook.com/communitystandards#hate-speech.

94–95 "The Twitter Rules," Twitter, accessed September 7, 2018, https://help
.twitter.com/en/rules-and-policies/twitter-rules.

97 Christian Picciolini, *White American Youth: My Descent into America's Most
Violent Hate Movement—and How I Got Out* (New York: Hachette Books,
2017), 3.

98–99 Christian Picciolini, "My Descent into America's Neo-Nazi Movement—
and How I Got Out," lecture, TEDxMileHigh, November 2017, https://
www.ted.com/talks/christian_picciolini_my_descent_into_america_s
_neo_nazi_movement_and_how_i_got_out.

100 Christian Picciolini, quoted in Janaya Williams and Stacey Vanek Smith, "A
Reformed White Nationalist Speaks Out on Charlottesville," *NPR*, August
13, 2017, https://www.npr.org/2017/08/13/543259499/a-reformed-white
-nationalist-speaks-out-on-charlottesville.

100 Ervin Staub, quoted in Sharon Jayson, "Why People Join Hate Groups,"
Inquirer.net, August 30, 2017, https://usa.inquirer.net/6296/people-join
-hate-groups.

101 Tony McAleer, quoted in Jayson.

101 Deborah Gilboa, quoted in Meghan Holohan, "White Supremacists Recruit
Teens by Making them Feel Someone Cares," *Today*, August 21, 2017,
https://www.today.com/parents/white-supremacists-prey-vulnerable-kids
-exploit-weakness-t115276.

101 Picciolini, quoted in Marteen Mokalla, "I'm a Former Neo-Nazi. Don't
Ignore the Threat of White Extremism," Vox, February 27, 2017, https://
www.vox.com/videos/2017/2/27/14738170/former-neo-nazi-dont-ignore
-threat-of-white-extremism-picciolini.

102 Kathleen M. Blee, quoted in "A Way Forward from Hate: An Interview
with Angela King," Life After Hate, November 2, 2017, https://www
.lifeafterhate.org/blog/2018/6/26/a-way-forward-from-hate-an-interview
-with-angela-king.

102 Peter Simi, quoted in Dahleen Glanton, "How the Seeds of Hate Are
Sown," *Chicago Tribune*, August 24, 2017, http://www.chicagotribune.com
/news/columnists/glanton/ct-hate-groups-dahleen-glanton-0824-20170823
-column.html.

103 A. J. Marsden, quoted in Elizabeth Chuck, "The Psychology of Hate
Groups: What Drives Someone to Join One," *NBC News*, August 16, 2017,
https://www.nbcnews.com/news/us-news/psychology-hate-groups-what
-drives-someone-join-one-n792941.

103 Robert Futrell, quoted in Jayson, "Hate Groups."

107 Mona Haydar, quoted in "After San Bernardino, This Couple Fought Islamophobia with Donuts and Conversation," Vox, January 11, 2017, https://www.vox.com/videos/2017/1/11/14226924/san-bernardino-islamophobia-sebastian-robins-mona-haydar-doughnuts.

110 Tammie Schnitzer, quoted in Claire Safran, "Not in Our Town," Redbook, November 1994, excerpts online at Facing History and Ourselves, accessed April 10, 2018, https://www.facinghistory.org/holocaust-and-human-behavior/chapter-12/not-our-town.

110 Anonymous, quoted in Safran.

111 Margaret MacDonald, quoted in Safran.

111 Tony McAleer, quoted in Al Donato, "Former Skinhead Now Helps Others Leave Hate Groups," CBC, November 26, 2017, https://www.cbc.ca/cbcdocspov/features/former-skinhead-now-helps-others-leave-hate-groups.

112 Shane Johnson, quoted in Jay Reeves, "Former White Supremacists Help Others Leave Hate Groups," Associated Press, February 21, 2017, https://www.apnews.com/690ae31e52674a3c89aed5b7fadd109a.

112 Johnson, quoted in Reeves.

113 Angela King, quoted in Claire Bates, "I Was a Neo-Nazi. Then I Fell in Love with a Black Woman," BBC World Service, August 29, 2017, https://www.bbc.com/news/magazine-40779377.

113 Peter Simi, quoted in Francie Diep, "What We Can Learn from People Who Have Left White Supremacy Hate Groups," Pacific Standard, August 21, 2017, https://www.psmag.com/social-justice/what-we-can-learn-from-people-who-have-left-white-supremacy-groups.

114 Picciolini, quoted in Harrison Jacobs, "A Former White Supremacist Has a Potentially Unpopular Message for How to Stop Extremist Movements," Business Insider, August 26, 2017, http://www.businessinsider.com/white-supremacist-nationalist-movements-how-to-stop-2017-8.

114 Michael Kimmel, quoted in Wes Enzinna, "Inside the Radical, Uncomfortable Movement to Reform White Supremacists," Mother Jones, July/August 2018, https://www.motherjones.com/politics/2018/07/reform-white-supremacists-shane-johnson-life-after-hate/.

114 Frank Meeink, quoted in Salvatore Caputo, "'Recovering Skinhead' Describes His Journey," Jewish News, February 14, 2017, https://www.jewishaz.com/community/recovering-skinhead-describes-his-journey/article_7f79f676-f313-11e6-bd7e-2f1fab63b709.html.

115 Jim Hand, "Racist Graffiti Found at Attleboro High School," *Attleboro (MA) Sun Chronicle*, November 16, 2016, http://www.thesunchronicle .com/news/local_news/racist-graffiti-found-at-attleboro-high-school /article_b64055bf-4fcf-5d9c-a58d-cc66d79789ff.html.

115 Iffa Sugrio, quoted in Jim Hand, "Attleboro High Students Combat Hateful Graffiti with Notes of Love," *Atteboro (MA) Sun Chronicle*, December 20, 2016, http://www.thesunchronicle.com/news/local_news/attleboro-high -students-combat-hateful-graffiti-with-notes-of-love/article_1c68e8bd-37c3 -59a7-980e-e874bf694978.html.

115 Dylan Ilkowitz, quoted in Hand.

116 Sarah Anthony, quoted in Safran, "Not in Our Town."

117 Dylan Brogan, "Swastikas and 'Trump Rules' Found on Plaque outside Madison Synagogue Building," *Isthmus*, September 20, 2017, http://www .isthmus.com/news/news/swastikas-trump-rules-plaque-madison -synagogue/.

118 Frank Meeink, quoted in Anna Almendrala and Melissa Jeltsen, "They Left White Power Behind. Now, They're Haunted by Its Resurgence," Huffington Post, August 22, 2017, https://www.huffingtonpost.com/entry /they-left-white-power-behind-now-theyre-haunted-by-its-resurgence_us _5996ef1ae4b0a2608a6bd028.

119–120 Heidi Beirich, quoted in "As Racial Hate Groups Rise, Strategies to Shut Them Down," *PBS News Hour*, March 25, 2016, https://www.pbs.org /newshour/show/as-racial-hate-groups-rise-strategies-to-shut-them-down.

120 Ziad Ahmed, quoted in Larisa Epatko, "'It's Hard to Hate Someone You Know': Teen's Website Battles Bias," *PBS News Hour*, June 26, 2015, https:// www.pbs.org/newshour/nation/teens-website-battles-bias.

138 "About," *re*defy, accessed September 14, 2018, https://redefy.org/about/.

SELECTED BIBLIOGRAPHY

"Anti-Jewish Legislation in Prewar Germany." *Holocaust Encyclopedia*. Accessed June 4, 2018. https://www.ushmm.org/wlc/en/article.php?ModuleId=10005681.

Carpenter, Zoë. "A History of Hate Rock from Johnny Rebel to Dylann Roof." *Nation*, June 23, 2015. https://www.thenation.com/article/a-history-of-hate-rock -from-johnny-rebel-to-dylann-roof/.

"The Civil Rights Movement." Documents of Freedom. Accessed August 31, 2018. https://www.docsoffreedom.org/student/readings/the-civil-rights-movement.

Couch, Christina. "Recovering from Hate." *PBS: Nova Next*, July 29, 2015. https:// www.pbs.org/wgbh/nova/next/body/hatred/.

Enzinna, Wes. "Inside the Radical, Uncomfortable Movement to Reform White Supremacists." *Mother Jones*, July/August 2018. https://www.motherjones.com /politics/2018/07/reform-white-supremacists-shane-johnson-life-after-hate/.

Florida, Richard. "Where Hate Groups Are Concentrated in the U.S." CityLab, March 15, 2018. https://www.citylab.com/equity/2018/03/where-hate-groups-are -concentrated-in-the-us/555689/.

Grossman, Ron. "'Swastika War': When the Neo-Nazis Fought in Court to March in Skokie." *Chicago Tribune*, March 10, 2017. http://www.chicagotribune.com/news /opinion/commentary/ct-neo-nazi-skokie-march-flashback-perspec-0312-20170310 -story.html.

"Hate on Social Media." Southern Poverty Law Center. Accessed February 8, 2018. https://www.splcenter.org/issues/hate-and-extremism.

Heim, Joe. "Recounting a Day of Rage, Hate, Violence and Death." *Washington Post*, August 14, 2017. https://www.washingtonpost.com/graphics/2017/local /charlottesville-timeline/?utm_term=.b9c544113c12.

Imlay, Ashley. "Geography of Hate: U. Study Examines Hate Groups Based on Religion." *Salt Lake City Deseret News*, February 11, 2018. https://www.deseretnews .com/article/900010002/geography-of-hate-u-study-examines-hate-groups-based-on -region.html.

"Immigration Timeline." The Statue of Liberty—Ellis Island Foundation. Accessed February 28, 2018. https://www.libertyellisfoundation.org/immigration-timeline.

Jayson, Sharon. "Why People Join Hate Groups." *Inquirer.net*, August 30, 2017. https://usa.inquirer.net/6296/people-join-hate-groups.

Katel, Peter. "Hate Groups." *CQ Researcher*, May 8, 2009. http://library.cqpress.com /cqresearcher/document.php?id=cqresrre2009050800.

Kinney, Alison. "How the Klan Got Its Hood." *New Republic*, January 8, 2016. https://www.newrepublic.com/article/127242/klan-got-hood.

Lopez, German. "The Sneaky Language Today's Politicians Use to Get Away with Racism and Sexism." Vox, February 1, 2016. https://www.vox.com/2016/2/1/10889138/coded-language-thug-bossy.

———. "Why It's So Hard to Prosecute a Hate Crime." Vox, May 23, 2017. https://www.vox.com/identities/2017/4/10/15183902/hate-crime-trump-law.

McCoy, Terrence. "I Don't Know How You Got This Way." *Washington Post*, February 23, 2018. https://www.washingtonpost.com/news/local/wp/2018/02/23/feature/i-dont-know-how-you-got-this-way-a-young-neo-nazi-reveals-himself-to-his-family/?undefined=&utm_term=.9524172f3bf5&wpisrc=nl_most&wpmm=1.

McCreesh, Shawn. "Antifa and the 'Alt-Left': Everything You Need to Know." *Rolling Stone*, August 18, 2017. https://www.rollingstone.com/culture/news/antifa-and-the-alt-left-everything-you-need-to-know-w498420.

Moser, Bob. "The Left's Supporting Role in American Hate Theater." *New Republic*, August 7, 2017. https://www.newrepublic.com/article/143933/lefts-supporting-role-american-hate-theater.

Picciolini, Christian. *White American Youth: My Descent into America's Most Violent Hate Movement—and How I Got Out.* New York: Hachette Books, 2017.

Robinson, B. A. "Hate Crime Arguments Pro & Con. Civil Rights Concerns about These Laws." Religious Tolerance, April 29, 2009. http://www.religioustolerance.org/hom_hat5.htm.

Rogers, Michelle. *The State of Hate in America: A Study of Hate Group Permeation in the United States by State.* CUNY Academic Works, graduate thesis, 2018. https://academicworks.cuny.edu/gc_etds/2474 .

Rosenblatt, Roger. "Their Finest Minute." *New York Times*, July 3, 1994. https://www.nytimes.com/1994/07/03/magazine/their-finest-minute.html.

Rothman, Joshua. "When Bigotry Paraded through the Streets." *Atlantic*, December 4, 2016. https://www.theatlantic.com/politics/archive/2016/12/second-klan/509468/.

Sankin, Aaron. "The Hate Report: How White Supremacists Recruit Online." Reveal, January 12, 2018. https://www.revealnews.org/blog/the-hate-report-how-white-supremacists-recruit-online/.

Simi, Peter, and Robert Futrell. *American Swastika: Inside the White Power Movement's Hidden Spaces of Hate.* 2nd ed. Latham, MD: Rowman & Littlefield, 2015.

Skutsch, Carl. "The History of White Supremacy in America." *Rolling Stone*, August 19, 2017. https://www.rollingstone.com/politics/features/the-history-of-white-supremacy-in-america-w498334.

Spies, Mike. "Exiled from Westboro: Leaving America's Most Hated Church." Vocativ, December 1, 2014. https://www.vocativ.com/usa/us-politics/westboro-baptist-church/index.html.

Suler, John. *The Psychology of Cyberspace*. Accessed September 24, 2018. http://www
.truecenterpublishing.com/psycyber/psycyber.html.

Tanvi, Misra. "United States of Muslim Hate." CityLab, March 9, 2018. https://www
.citylab.com/equity/2018/03/anti-muslim-hate-crime-map/555134/.

Underwood, Alexia. "What Most Americans Get Wrong about Islamophobia." Vox,
April 6, 2018. https://www.vox.com/2018/4/6/17169448/trump-islamophobia
-muslims-islam-black-lives-matter.

Weigel, Moira. "Political Correctness: How the Right Invented a Phantom Enemy."
Guardian (US ed.), November 30, 2016. https://www.theguardian.com/us-news
/2016/nov/30/political-correctness-how-the-right-invented-phantom-enemy
-donald-trump.

Wolf, Sherry. "Stonewall: The Birth of Gay Power." *International Socialist Review* 63
(January 2009). https://www.isreview.org/issue/63/stonewall-birth-gay-power.

FURTHER INFORMATION

BOOKS

Abramovitz, Melissa. *Hate Crimes in America*. Minneapolis: Abdo, 2017.

Behnke, Alison Marie. *Racial Profiling: Everyday Inequality*. Minneapolis:
Twenty-First Century Books, 2017.

Davidson, Danica. *Everything You Need to Know about Hate Crimes*. New York:
Rosen, 2018.

Doeden, Matt. *A Marked Man: The Assassination of Malcom X*. Minneapolis:
Twenty-First Century Books, 2013.

Gerstenfeld, Phyllis B. *Hate Crimes: Causes, Controls, and Controversies*. 4th ed.
Thousand Oaks, CA: Sage, 2018.

Higgins, Nadia Abushanab. *Feminism: Reinventing the F-Word*. Minneapolis:
Twenty-First Century Books, 2016.

Hurt, Avery Elizabeth. *Coping with Hate and Intolerance*. New York: Rosen, 2018.

Keyser, Amber J. *No More Excuses: Dismantling Rape Culture*. Minneapolis:
Twenty-First Century Books, 2019.

Rutledge, Jill S. Zimmerman. *Prom: The Big Night Out*. Minneapolis: Twenty-First
Century Books, 2017.

Sethi, Arjun Singh, ed. *American Hate: Survivors Speak Out*. New York: New Press,
2018.

Waldron, Jeremy. *The Harm in Hate Speech.* Cambridge, MA: Harvard University Press, 2012.

Wittenstein, Vicki Oransky. *Reproductive Rights: Who Decides?* Minneapolis: Twenty-First Century Books, 2016.

FILMS

The Black Panthers: Vanguard of the Revolution. Directed by Stanley Nelson. *PBS, Independent Lens*, 2016. https://www.pbs.org/independentlens/films/the-black -panthers-vanguard-of-the-revolution/.
This feature-length documentary explores the turbulent history of the Black Panther Party and its significance in the history of black Americans fighting for equality and racial justice. It won an NAACP Image Award for Outstanding Documentary.

Boys Don't Cry. Directed by Kimberly Peirce. Beverly Hills, CA: Fox Searchlight Pictures, 1999.
This film is a dramatization of the life of Brandon Teena, a trans man in Nebraska who was the victim of a brutal hate crime. Hilary Swank won an Academy Award for Best Actress for her performance as Teena.

Documenting Hate: Charlottesville. PBS, *Frontline*/ProPublica, 2018. https://www.pbs .org/wgbh/frontline/film/documenting-hate-charlottesville/.
This episode of the PBS series *Frontline* investigates the white supremacists and neo-Nazis involved in the 2017 Unite the Right rally in Charlottesville, Virginia.

Hate in America. New York: Peacock Productions, 2016. Investigation Discovery. https://www.investigationdiscovery.com/tv-shows/hate-in-america/.
This three-part documentary investigates modern-day racism in the United States, with individual episodes focusing on the Ku Klux Klan, white supremacism, and domestic terrorism.

The Hate That Hate Produced. Produced by Mike Wallace and Louis Lomax. News Beat/WNTA-TV, 1959.
Renowned journalist Mike Wallace narrates this classic documentary, originally aired in five parts. It focuses on the Nation of Islam, black nationalism, and its leaders—including Malcom X and Louis X (Louis Farrakhan).

Hate Thy Neighbor. Vice Europe TV, 2017–2018. Viceland. https://www.viceland .com/en_us/show/hate-thy-neighbor.
In this sixteen-part documentary TV series, comedian Jamali Maddix tours the world to interview members of extremist hate groups.

Not in Our Town. PBS, 1995–2012. https://www.pbs.org/show/not-our-town/.
This series of PBS specials documents how citizens of various small towns work to prevent hate and intolerance in their communities. The original 1995 special,

Not in Our Town, detailed how the citizens of Billings, Montana, responded to the influx of hate groups. Subsequent specials include *Not in Our Town II* (1996), *Not in Our Town Northern California: When Hate Happens Here* (2005), *Not in Our Town: Light into Darkness* (2011), and *Not in Our Town: Class Actions* (2012).

An Outrage. Teaching Tolerance, 2017. https://www.tolerance.org/classroom-resources /film-kits/an-outrage.
This documentary film, by Hannah Ayers and Lance Warren for students in grades 9 to 12, focuses on lynching in the American South. It looks at the topic through the eyes of community activists, scholars, and descendants of lynching victims.

Third Reich: The Rise and Fall. Directed by Seth Skundrick and Nicole Rittenmeyer. History Channel/New Animal Productions, 2010.
A two-part documentary, originally aired on the History Channel, looks at Hitler's Nazi Germany through rarely seen films of people who were there in the 1920s, 1930s, and 1940s. It uses home movies, Nazi propaganda films, and other contemporaneous media to document this period of German history.

WEBSITES

American Civil Liberties Union (ACLU)
https://www.aclu.org/
The home page of the American Civil Liberties Union offers information on First Amendment freedoms as well as many other rights issues. Check out your rights and how the ACLU is working to defend them. Learn how you can get involved in civil rights causes.

Anti-Defamation League (ADL)
https://www.adl.org
The Anti-Defamation League monitors and fights anti-Semitism, bigotry, and hate crimes around the world. The website includes a wealth of material on hate groups, hate speech, and hate crimes, including an interactive H.E.A.T. (Hate, Extremism, Anti-Semitism, Terrorism) map that tracks incidences of hate, extremism, anti-Semitism, and terror. The site also includes a database of symbols used by hate groups, as well as a collection of news articles and research tools. Additional resources include numerous tools for fighting hate, including books and other literature, conversation-starting tools, and bullying and cyberbullying.

Center for the Study of Hate and Extremism
https://csbs.csusb.edu/hate-and-extremism-center
This nonpartisan research and policy center, part of California State University, San Bernardino, examines the ways that bigotry, terrorism, and other forms of hate deny civil rights to people on the basis of race, ethnicity, gender, and other characteristics. The center conducts research into hate crimes and terrorism, including releasing annual hate crime analyses and reports.

The Cult Education Institute

https://www.culteducation.com

This is the website for a nonprofit organization devoted to studying cults (including hate groups) and helping people leave them. It aggregates data from a variety of sources and monitors and reports on hate groups. The site includes a large list of hate groups, with links to information about each and their activities.

FBI: Hate Crimes

https://www.fbi.gov/investigate/civil-rights/hate-crimes

This site explains the FBI's role in monitoring and combating hate crimes. It also includes links to hate crime statistics, by year, and resources related to hate groups and civil rights abuses.

Free Radicals Project

https://www.freeradicals.org

This organization, led by former hate group leader Christian Picciolini, is dedicated to helping hate group members disengage from their lives of hate. Visitors can use the online form at this website if they need help in leaving a hate group.

Legacy Museum

https://museumandmemorial.eji.org/museum

The Legacy Museum is in Montgomery, Alabama, on the site of a former warehouse where black people were enslaved. The museum commemorates the history of slavery and racial intolerance—including hate groups and hate crimes—in the United States. Also at this location is the National Memorial for Justice and Peace, which is a memorial to the more than forty-four hundred black American men, women, and children who were lynched, burned alive, drowned, shot, and beaten to death by white mobs between 1877 and 1950. The website includes information about both the museum and monument and the events that inspired the creation of both.

Life After Hate

https://www.lifeafterhate.org

This organization, run by ex-hate group members, is devoted to helping current members leave hate groups and hate group ideology. The organization has tens of thousands of supporters and has helped more than one hundred people leave hate groups. The website offers stories from people who have left the world of hate, programs to spread the organization's message, and a form that people can fill out if they need help leaving a hate group.

Partners Against Hate

http://www.partnersagainsthate.org

This organization, a collaboration between the Anti-Defamation League, the Leadership Conference Education Fund, and the Center for the Prevention of Hate Violence, offers online and printable resources that support the fight against hate crimes and violence perpetrated by middle- and high-school youth. Especially useful is the group's downloadable *Helping Youth Resist Bias and Hate Program Activity Guide*, which includes information, advice, and resources for recognizing, responding to, and resisting hate and hate groups.

Redefy
https://www.redefy.org
This is a site by teenagers and for teenagers, designed to promote tolerance and fight discrimination and hate. The site's stated goal is to "boldly defy stereotypes, embrace acceptance, redefine our perspectives positively, and create an active community." The site shares stories and photos of people of different races, religions, and genders from around the world.

Simon Wiesenthal Center
http://www.wiesenthal.com
According to its mission statement, the Simon Wiesenthal Center is a global human rights organization that researches the Holocaust from a modern and historic context. It promotes human rights and confronts anti-Semitism as well as other forms of hate and terrorism. The organization, named after famed human rights activist Simon Wiesenthal, also funds the Museum of Tolerance, in Los Angeles, California, and Jerusalem, Israel. The website features links to these museums, as well as news about anti-Semitic and hate group activities around the world.

Southern Poverty Law Center (SPLC)
https://www.splcenter.org
The Southern Poverty Law Center monitors and fights hate groups and hate crimes across the United States. Among other resources, the organization's website includes the Extremist Files, a database of prominent extremists and extremist organizations; the *Hatewatch* blog, which monitors activities of the American radical right; the *Intelligence Report*, a periodical devoted to monitoring the radical right; and the Hate Map, an infographic that tracks all known hate groups in the United States.

Understanding and Overcoming Hate
https://www.overcominghateportal.org
This site is dedicated to understanding and overcoming hate. It includes a variety of tools, content, links, and other resources related to hate speech, hate groups, and hate crimes. To help overcome hate, the site focuses on prevention, education, intervention, and social advances—with links to multiple organizations, programs, papers, and coalitions.

INDEX

ABOUT THE AUTHOR

Michael Miller is a prolific and best-selling writer. He has written more than two hundred nonfiction books on a variety of topics, including technology, music, and business. Besides writing books and articles, Miller is a consultant, speaker, and drummer. He lives with his wife, several stepchildren, and six grandchildren in the Twin Cities area of Minnesota. *Fake News* and *Exposing Hate* are his first books for young adult readers.

PHOTO ACKNOWLEDGMENTS